Safety instructions (do *not* remove)
Instructions de sécurité (ne pas enlever)
Sicherheitsan- weisungen (nicht zu entfernen)

English

1. Do *not* open the book.
2. Ensure that you are not holding the book in a naked flame or near a sulphuric acid-throwing machine.
3. Ensure that what you are holding *is* a book and not a deadly fish (piranha, hammer-head shark, African naughty minnow etc).
4. Before commencement of reading acquaint yourself fully with the location of the back cover (A) and the front cover (A), so that these can be closed quickly in time of emergency.
5. Always hold the book away from the face (A).
6. When reading loosen all articles of clothing.
7. Loosen the clothing even more.
8. Loosen bras and suspender belts especially.
9. Loosen my clothing.
10. Now hold my ———— and tickle ————.

Français

1. Ne tenez [...]
2. [...]nue ni [...]itriol.
3. [...]ous
4. Avant [...] la lecture repérez le dos [...], ainsi que la face (A) de la couverture, afin de les pouvoir fermer rapidement en cas d'urgence.
5. Tenez le livre toujours à quelque distance du visage (A).
6. Pendant la lecture desserrez tous vos vêtements.
7. Desserrez vos vêtements encore plus.
8. Desserrez votre soutien-gorge et votre gaine de hanches en particulier.
9. Desserrez mes vêtements.
10. Maintenant tenez mon ———— et chatouillez ————.

Deutsch

1. Das Buch nicht öffnen.*
2. Vergewissen Sie sich das Sie das Buch nicht in eine nackte Flamme halten oder in der Nähe eines Schwefelsäurewerfers.
3. Vergewissen Sie sich dass das was Sie halten ein Buch ist und nicht ein tödlicher Fisch (eine Piranha, ein Hammerhai, oder eine freche afrikanische Elritze u.s.w.).
4. Bevor Sie zu lesen beginnen, machen Sie sich vollstens mit der Lage der Rückseite (A) und der Vorderseite (A) bekannt, so dass Sie diese im Notfall schnellstens schliessen können.
5. Halten Sie das Buch immer vom Gesicht entfernt (A).
6. Offnen Sie alle Kleidungsstücke beim Lesen.
7. Alle Kleidungsstücke noch mehr öffnen.
8. Insbesondere Büstenhalter und Strumpfhaltergürtel.
9. Öffnen Sie meine Kleider.
10' Halten Sie mein ———— und kitzeln Sie ————.

Reading positions
Positions de lecture
Lesehaltungen

English

1. The safety reading position (A).
2. Emergency reading position (A) with the knees drawn up into the stomach and the head buried between the thighs, holding the book between heel of left foot (A) and instep of right foot (A). Turn the pages with second and third toes of foot (A) and nose (A).

Français

1. La position de lecture de sécurité (A).
2. Position de lecture d'urgence: les genoux contre le ventre, la tête entre les cuisses; tenez le livre entre le talon gauche (A) et le cou-de-pied droit (A). Feuilletez avec deuxième et troisième orteils du pied (A) et avec le nez (A).

Deutsch

1. Die Sicherheitslesehaltung (A).
2. Notlesehaltung (A) mit den Knien zum Bauch gezogen und den Kopf zwischen den Schenkeln; halten Sie das Buch zwischen der Ferse des linken Fusses (A) und dem Spann des rechten Fusses (A). Blättern Sie mit der zweiten und dritten Zehe des Fusses (A) und der Nase (A) um.

In the event of a reading emergency
En cas d'urgence pendant la lecture
Im Falle einer Lesenot

English

(e.g. fire, rape, Des O'Connor Show etc.)

1. Close the book firmly.
2. Scream.
3. Hit it/him/the show with the book.
4. Remove *all* dangerous articles—watches, jewellery, sharp money, heavy uncrossed cheques etc—and place them in the bag marked 'Air Methuen, 12 New Fetter Lane' which you will find under every page.
5. Should you land in the sea while reading this book, press page 42 which will expand into a fully inflatable life raft, with a three-week supply of curry.

Français

(par ex. incendie, viol, Des O'Connor Show et caetera)

1. Fermez vite le livre.
2. Criez.
3. Frappez-la/le/le show avec le livre.
4. Enlevez tous objets dangereux—montres, bijouterie, argent pointu, chèques ouverts trop lourds, et caetera—et m[ettez-les dans le sac marqué] 'Air Me[thuen, 12 New Fetter Lane'] que vou[s ...]
5. Dans [...] cours [...] page 42 [...] de sauv[...] cari suf[...]

Deutsch

(z.B. Feuer, Vergewaltigung, Des O'Connor Show u.s.w.)

1. Schliessen Sie das Buch fest zu.
2. Schreien. Sie.
3. Schlagen Sie es/ihn/die Show mit dem Buch.
4. Entfernen Sie alle gefährlichen Gegenstände-Uhren, Schmuckstücke, [...]ere ungekreuzte [...]d stecken Sie sie [...]r Aufschrift 'Air [...]Fetter Lane' die [...]e befindet. [...]rend Sie dieses [...] landen, drücken [...]sich in ein Ret-[...]öchigem Vorrat [...] wird.

a

b

English

It is advisable to send your valuables to Air Methuen anyway. More people are robbed while reading than you think. Stop laughing. It's true.

*This instruction has been deleted. It was a silly instruction—unworkable in practice and unethical in intent. We sincerely apologize for this instruction. The person responsible has since been disembowelled. Yours sincerely, Air Methuen.
We sincerely apologize for any embarrassment that may have been caused by instructions 6, 7, 8 and 9. We now realize that they were unnecessary and the product of a disordered mind. The man who wrote them has since been guillotined and his knees stapled together. Yours sincerely, Air Methuen.

Français

En tout[...] conseill[...] envoyer [...] de vol[...] lecture des livres que vous ne pensez. Ne rigolez pas. C'est vrai.

*Cette instruction a été biffée. Ce fut une instruc[...] et immoral[...] nous excus[...] de cette [...] responsabl[...] dévoué, Ai[r...] Nous nous excusons since[...] toute gêne qui aurait pû résulter des instructions 6, 7, 8 et 9. Nous nous rendons compte maintenant qu'elles n'étaient pas nécessaires et qu'elles sont le produit d'un esprit malade. Quant à l'homme qui les a écrites on l'a guillotiné d'abord et puis on lui a broché les genoux au fil de fer. Votre tout dévoué, Air Methuen.

Deutsch

[...]tsam ihre Wert-[...]uen zu senden. [...] denken werden [...]t. Lache Nicht.

*Diese Anweisung wurde gestrichen. Es war eine blöde Anweisung—unmöglich in der Praxis und im [...]moralisch. Wir entschul-[...]ufrichtig für diese An-[...]er verantwortlichen Per-[...]seitdem der Bauch auf-[...]ldigen uns aufrichtig für jegliche Peinlichkeit die Sie durch Anweisungen 6, 7, 8 und 9 erlitten haben. Wir sind uns jetzt klar dass sie unnötig und das Werk eines Geisteskranken waren. Der Mann, der sie verfasst hat, ist seitdem unter das Fallbeil gekommen und seine Knie sind zusammengeheftet worden. Hochachtungsvoll Air Methuen.

Hello boys and girls. I'm the old story teller. Today I'd like to tell you about an amazing land in a far, far off place, where no one ever has the wobbles.

In this fabulous land even the clouds are free to go where they please.

On Sundays they can go in small, well-chaperoned groups to the vast plasterboard cities that pierce the sun.

Near these cities grow shining black mountains. And near these mountains live bulging purple seas full of fishes of every known race, creed, and/or colour.

High above the water stand strange birds whose feet never quite reach the ground.

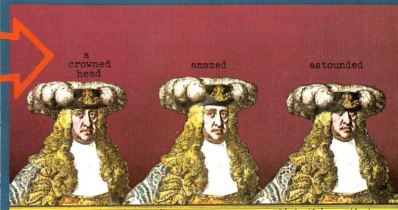

a crowned head   amazed   astounded

And on their wings live small brown roundish things that have amazed and astounded the crowned heads of Europe for over 300 years.

The birds are not the only things that don't touch the ground in this strange land. Unfortunately the topsoil is very light, too light in fact to stay in contact with the ground and so it floats 3 feet above it.

3 feet

a

This would not be so bad, but for the fact that the people of this land do everything by fours, including walking on them.

And so, most of the people choose to live in the vast plasterboard cities where topsoil is not allowed - except a bit on Thursdays and on another day they don't have a name for. As I said, I would like to tell you about this amazing land, but the bastards who put this book together have only given me two pages and insist I finish so they can get on with the pretentious so-called funny stuff they've prepared. If I was younger and still had my health they wouldn't dare treat me like this. I'd have my own book. But there you go just because I smell funny and can't make it to the toilet in time. Punks.

BIGGLES IS EXTREMELY SILLY

(1938)

Squadron-Leader Bigglesworth paused for a moment outside the Wingco's office. He had been called back from leave three days early, and this didn't happen unless things were really wrong.

He knocked and went in. Came out, knocked, went in, knocked again, went in, came out, knocked, went in again, knocked again from the inside, came out, knocked from the outside, went in, knocked again, came out, did a little jump, knocked, went "Ee-aw!", knocked again, jumped, ran out, knocked, came in again with a waste-paper basket over his head, jumped, knocked, went out, knocked and entered the dimly-lit office. "There you are Bigglesworth," said the Wingco with just a trace of annoyance. Only a trace, not a fully-fledged burst of anger or a downright bitch about Biggles being late or a swingeing attack on the punctuality of Air Force personnel or even a snide dig at Biggles' general attitude or an irritation that he was forced, by his seniority, to be in a position where he was potentially a target for the general feelings of bitterness prevalent in the upper echelons of Fighter Command due to a combination of fatigue, long hours and the severe strain imposed on any man's self-control by the duties and responsibilities inherent in his rank, nor was there any hint. . . .

BIGGLES AND THE NAUGHTY THINGS
(1941)

Squadron-Leader Bigglesworth walked purposefully across the tarmac. It was a cold, grey, November morning, and the mist was drifting across the desolate airfield. Biggles clambered onto the wing of the waiting Jupiter and lowered himself into the cockpit.

"Weather looks dicey," observed Ginger drily.

"The sooner we get off the better," murmured Algy, "I'd rather see this bally fog from topsides."

"Shut up, the pair of you," snapped Biggles, "and hand me the substances."

"Oh, you're not going to smoke, are you Biggles?" queried Algy.

"It's such a bally awful smell," added Ginger ruefully.

Biggles took some resin from the First-Aid box, and working away with his pen-knife, soon had enough to fill a generous joint. He lit up briskly, and slamming the Jupiter into full throttle, taxied into the drifting mist, through the hangar, the W.A.A.F. Canteen, a car park, a Social Centre, a model agency and an art-book publisher's delivery depot.

Suddenly he was airborne. Algy breathed a sigh of relief and eased himself out of the co-pilot's seat.

"Oh, it's so hot in here," Algy declared evenly.

He began to unzip his flying jacket and soon stood naked in the faint glow of the altometer.

Ginger blushed hotly.

Algy returned his blush curtly.

Biggles also turned red and blushed and threw the twin-engined Jupiter into a tight turn over the airfield.

"Does my body offend you, Biggles?" queried Algy sharply.

Biggles said nothing. His drug-ravaged features showed no glimmer of emotion. His lips were set, his dilated pupils looked neither to right nor left, his hands gripped the joystick.

Suddenly out of the clouds, directly ahead of them, Ginger glimpsed the red flash of the Heinkel fighter.

"Look it's von Richthofen," he cried excitedly.

"Get your clothes on, Algy," murmured Biggles curtly.

"Shan't," returned Algy, teasingly.

"He's coming at us out of the sun!" yelled Ginger anxiously.

"Put your bloody trousers on, Algy," repeated Biggles grimly.

But it was too late, von Richthofen came nearer and nearer. Soon he was in the cockpit.

"My God we're done for," screamed Ginger.

"Aha! all ready are vee!" shouted von Richthofen, tearing off his flying suit.

Soon the little Jupiter monoplane powered by two 770 h.p. Cyclone engines was rocking from side to side, as the dastardly German wreaked his awful revenge on the drug-crazed British lads. . . .

Hello. If you would like to buy the film rights for this page they are still available, at least up to the point of publication they were available. Obviously if we've sold the film rights to this page since publication then they will no longer be available, unless of course you make a better offer than the one we have accepted already – that is, provided we have sold them already. We might not have done. They might still be available. However if they *have* been sold, there is still a chance you can increase the offer, providing of course we haven't exchanged contracts with the people who might have made the initial purchase, and in that way YOU can have the film rights to this page. If, of course we have exchanged contracts then you still have a chance through hidden clauses or tricky loops in the contracts which may make it possible for us to dodge the first agreement legally.

So, having made this offer you can now sit back content with your new 'property' as the film people call these things. Of course, you are going to ask how you can be sure that once having bought the film rights from us for this page, we won't then sell them off again to the next highest bidder or through a tricky loop in the contract do you out of your rights. Well, you can't. That's the film world. You might as well accept that from the beginning and get a good lawyer. But for a while, at least, YOU can be the proud owner of the film rights for this page.

What are you getting for your money? You might well ask. And indeed you would be quite foolish if you, or your legal adviser, didn't at some stage in the various complicated negotiations involved in buying film rights, ask such a question. Well the answer is very simple. YOU would be getting the exclusive film rights for this page IN ITS ENTIRETY, including the page number and the heading, to film the contents in whatever manner you thought fit, to hire and fire Directors to film this page for you to your satisfaction, to employ any amount of scriptwriters to rewrite this page to your notion of how best it could be filmed, to engage film stars or actors to play in the screen version of this page and to have dinner with you and to lease the distribution rights of the finished film to any company that you so wished, Ranks, ABC or even Sainsbury's.

So now it's up to you to decide whether you should branch out into the film production business where you could rub shoulders with Harry Saltzman, or Cubby Broccoli – INDEED you might even be competing against THEM for the film rights of this very page. (Always presuming of course that Harry or Cubby haven't already taken out an option on this page, since publication of this book, in which case it would be up to you either to increase their offer or to buy out their option. Exciting world isn't it?)

One or two things that might just worry you if you are hesitating whether or not to splash out and try and buy the film rights for this page or not; Eyre Methuen do not own the film rights at all and in fact would make no money whatsoever if YOU made ten films from this page, or indeed if you turned it into a television series. So that's them right out of it. And serves 'em right too for making such bad deals in the first place. (Of course they are perfectly entitled to try and buy the film rights for themselves just as you are, but that's a different kettle of fish.)

Secondly PYTHON PRODUCTIONS who are at the moment the sole owners of the film rights for this page (providing we haven't sold them since publication or even yesterday) would insist on suitable billing in any credits of YOUR film, i.e. if you decided to make this page a vehicle for Ursula Andress and Michael Caine then we should compel you by law to make your credits run

Ursula Andress and Michael Caine in YOUR production of (Whatever title you decide is commercial) Based on the original page 6 of 'The Brand New Monty Python Bok'.

SO having made up your mind here's what to do. Write to *Python Productions*, enclosing a cheque with your serious offer for the film rights of this page. And we shall write back quite soon and tell you if your bid has been successful or whether we have already done a deal with Harry and Cubby. So good luck, and remember ANYONE can be a film producer, all you need is money and a certain vicious ruthlessness. Be seeing you.

Here are some film stars you might like to cast – in your film of this page: Rock Hudson, Jane Fonda, Rolf Harris, Steve McQueen, Ali McGraw

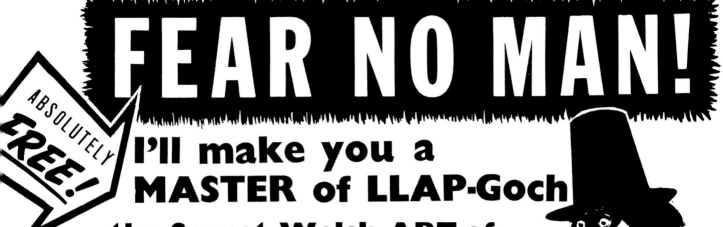

FEAR NO MAN!

ABSOLUTELY FREE!

I'll make you a MASTER of LLAP-Goch

... the Secret Welsh ART of SELF DEFENCE that requires NO INTELLIGENCE, STRENGTH or PHYSICAL courage

The FANTASTIC SECRETS of the SECRET world-famous method of SELF DEFENCE, kept secret for centuries because of their DEADLY POWER to MAIM, KILL, SMASH, BATTER, FRACTURE, CRUSH, DISMEMBER, CRACK, DISEMBOWEL, CRIPPLE, SNAP and HARM are now revealed to YOU in the English Language by a LLAP-GOCH master AT HIS OWN RISK, PROVIDED you promise to MAIM, CRUSH, DISEMBOWEL and so on ONLY in SELF DEFENCE.* *This is just to cover ourselves, as you will understand.*

WHY 'At his own risk'?

BECAUSE if his fellow masters of LLAP-GOCH DISCOVER his IDENTITY, they will PUNISH HIM SEVERELY for revealing the DEADLY secrets he had promised to keep SECRET, without giving them a piece of the ACTION, and also BECAUSE of the TERRIBLE risk of PUNISHMENT he runs under the Trades Description Act.

WHAT is LLAP-GOCH?

IT is THE most DEADLY form OF SECRET self-DEFENCE that HAS ever been widely advertised and available to EVERYONE.

WHY ALL the CAPITALS?

Because THE most likely kind OF person TO answer THIS sort OF advertisement HAS less trouble under-STANDING words if they ARE written in BIG letters.

WHAT is LLAP-GOCH again?

It is an ANCIENT Welsh ART based on a BRILLIANTLY simple I-D-E-A, which is a SECRET. The best form of DEFENCE is ATTACK (Clausewitz) and the most VITAL element of ATTACK is SURPRISE (Oscar HAMMERstein). Therefore . . . the BEST way to protect yourself AGAINST any ASSAILANT is to ATTACK him before he attacks YOU . . . Or *BETTER* . . . BEFORE the THOUGHT of doing so has EVEN OCCURRED TO HIM!!! SO YOU MAY BE ABLE TO RENDER YOUR ASSAILANT *UNCONSCIOUS* BEFORE he is EVEN aware of your very existence!

Banish Inadequacy

No longer need you feel WEAK, helpless, INDECISIVE NOT fascinating and ASHAMED of your genital dimensions. No more need you be out-manoeuvred in political debate!! GOOD BYE HUMILIATION, Wisecracking bullies, Karate experts, boxing champions, sarcastic vicars, traffic wardens; entire panzer divisions will melt to pulp as you master every situation without INADEQUACY. PROTECT YOUR LOVED ONES. You will no longer look pitiful and spotty to your GIRL FRIENDS when you leave some unsuspecting passer-by looking like four tins of cat-food! They will admire your MASTERY and DECISIVENESS and LACK OF INADEQUACY and will almost certainly let you put your HAND inside their BLOUSE out of sheer ADMIRATION. And after seeing more of your expert disabling they'll almost definitely go to bed with you, although obviously we can't ABSOLUTELY *guarantee* this, still it's extremely likely and would make learning LLAP-GOCH really worthwhile although legally we can't PROMISE anything.

Why WELSH Art?

LLAP-GOCH was developed in Wales because for the average Welshman, the best prospects of achieving a reasonable standard of living lie with the acquisition of the most efficient techniques of armed robbery.

HOW do I learn?

No, you mean 'How do *You* Learn'. I know already.

HOW do You Learn?

You receive ABSOLUTELY FREE your own special personal LLAP-GOCH Picture Book with hundreds of PHOTOGRAPHS and just a very few plain, clear and simple, easy to understand words.

Only a FOUR-SECOND WORK-OUT Each Day!

and you will be ready to HARM peopie
DEVELOP UP TO 38" BICEPS
GROW UP TO 12" TALLER
LOSE UP TO 40" OF FAT IN YOUR FIRST WORK-OUT!
PROLONG YOUR LIFE BY *UP TO* 1,000 YEARS

WHO IS THIS MAN? THIS is the LLAP-GOCH MASTER who will reveal to YOU ONLY the secret SECRETS of LLAP-GOCH HE IS A FULLY QUALIFIED leek-coloured BELT FIRST DAI MASTER and cares nothing for penal reform.

GO TO BED WITH *UP TO* ANY LUDICROUS NUMBER OF *GIRLS* YOU CARE TO THINK OF PROVIDING YOU REALIZE THIS STATEMENT IS QUITE MEANINGLESS AS THE PHRASE 'UP TO' CLEARLY INCLUDES THE NUMBER 'NOUGHT'

What Does it Cost?

This, like LLAP-GOCH, is a SECRET but you will find out sooner or later, don't worry.

Edward Woodward's Fish Page

★★★★★★★★★★★★★★★★ **Where The Stars Buy Fish** ★★★★★★★★★★★★★★★★

Edward Woodward – MacFisheries
Dorothy Lamour – MacFisheries
Ted Rodgers – MacFisheries
Bob Monkhouse – MacFisheries
Mireille Mathieu – MacFisheries
Dale Carnegie – MacFisheries
Rod Laver – MacFisheries; Rudman Fish Shops; the Ross Group of Fish Shops; Selfridge's Fish Counter; Harrod's Fish Counter; Derry & Tom's Fish Counter;

H. Samuels Fish Counter (Unknown – Ed.); Scanlon Bros (Fish) Ltd., Wimbledon; The Forest Hills Fish Shop, Forest Hills, New York, N.Y. State, U.S.A.; The French Open Hard Court Championships Fish Bar & Plaice Boutique (opp. changing rooms) Paris, France; 'On-The-Court' Express Fish Services.
Senator 'Tom' Eagleton – MacFisheries
George Harrison – MacFisheries
Reginald Bosanquet – MacFisheries
Edward Woodward again – MacFisheries

Fishing Map of the Murrumbidgee River

Useless Tips For Anglers

1) Be sure the carburettor and spark-plugs are cleaned before reassembly.
2) Make sure that the shelf is at right-angles to the fixing-joint (use Rawlplug 'cavity fixing screws').
3) Always check the bill for service charge.
4) Rods should be about 3 feet long and 6 inches thick, and covered with industrial plasti-laminate (Brit. Standard BS 635429) $\frac{1}{3}$–$\frac{2}{3}$ inch thick including sound-proofing.
4) Pike can pass on whooping-cough if you let them breathe over you.

5) Carp, bream and guppies usually know a lot of useful phone-numbers, so make sure you extract the maximum information from them before you bang their heads on the stone.
6) Never believe trout.
7) For landing salmon, a little lipstick and a new hairdo will increase the average angler's chances no end.
8) Angling does *not* make you blind.
9) Taking your boots off when you fish does *not* encourage the growth of the testicles.*

Other Things Edward Woodward Can Do

Act very well, Sing, Dance, Recite From Memory, Scuba-Diving, Yachting, Judo, Flying, Power-Gliding, Motor-Racing, Sail Single-Handed Round the World (if he tried).

* The only sure-fire way of increasing the size of your testicles is to fill in the form below:

- -

Initial Offer
I wish to buy £...... worth (min. investment £500) of Slater-Nazi Testicular Growth Bonds

*I am over 21 and understand I may never see my money again.
Signed: Mr/Mrs............... address...........*

The Python Book of Etiquette

*How to reply to an invitation
without farting. How to pour wine without farting. How to cope with a stiffy
at the Royal Garden Party. How to address a bishop without farting.*

The Python Book of Etiquette is designed to help out on those many social occasions when you feel awkward or embarrassed about the right kind of behaviour. For instance, meeting the Royal Family.

The Python Book of Etiquette

What To Do On Meeting The Royal Family

This depends largely on where you meet the Royal Family. If you meet the Royal Family in a surgical supply shop, it is best not to acknowledge them at all, as this will only lead to embarrassment on your part, and on the part of the Royal person or persons.* However, should you meet a member of the Royal Family in normal circumstances the etiquette is clear and simple. If you are wearing a hat or turban, remove it instantly, and hold it in your left hand, leaving your right hand free should the Royal Personage decide on manual contact. Going down on one knee would be very much appreciated, but in a crowded supermarket or shopping precinct this could cause a great deal of congestion and end up with you getting kicked over.

NEVER touch the Royal Family under any circumstances, unless you yourself have been touched by them – and even then keep your hands well above the waist. The correct way to address the Royal Family is 'Your Majesty' or 'Your Highness', and not 'Hello Graham'. NEVER ask the Royal Family a direct question. For instance, should you wish to ask Princess Marina where the swimming baths are, you must say: 'The swimming baths are near here', and hope that she will say: 'No, I think you're wrong, they're over half a mile away down Thorpe Road and turn right at Hepworth's' or: 'Yes, they are near here. There they are.' NEVER shout abuse or push or jostle the Royal Family, unless they attack you.

* *The same applies in garages, betting shops, cinema clubs and public toilets.*

Words Not To Say To The Queen

*'Miss', 'Madam', 'you there', 'blimey', 'sod it!',
'piss-artist', 'bottom', 'what?', 'come
again?', 'masturbation'.*

A Typical Conversation With The Queen

QUEEN: *Arise.*
ORDINARY MAN: *Thank you, your Majesty.*
QUEEN: *What brings you to Wolverhampton?*
ORDINARY MAN: *I have an aunt who lives near here – well in Wellington, actually, which is just about – (you will have lost the Queen's attention by now. She meets many people, so keep your sentences short and sharp.)*
QUEEN: *Well, I must be going away . . .*
ORDINARY MAN: *Goodbye, your Majesty.*
QUEEN: *Goodbye, my man.*

A Bad Conversation With The Queen

ORDINARY MAN: *Hello, I didn't recognize you.*
QUEEN: *But I am the Queen!*
ORDINARY MAN: *You don't look at all like you do on the stamps.*
QUEEN: *Don't you speak to me like that, you dirty little nonentity.*
ORDINARY MAN: *Can you help me change this wheel?*
QUEEN: *Shut your fat gob, you nasty little pile of wombat's do's.*
A Conversation like this could ruin your chances of an O.B.E.

Spotting The Royal Family

How to recognise them.

 *a Queen*

 *a Duke*

 *a Princess*

 *a Opossum*

 *a Prince*

 *a Corgi*

WARNING: one of these is not really royal

Famous first Drafts

1. Keats

Ode to a ~~Gynaecologist~~ Barman
~~Nightwatchman~~ Nightingale

My heart ~~goes ping!~~ aches
~~pour~~ aches

And a ~~toosy~~ drowsy numbness pains my sense

As though of ~~Watneys~~ Hemlock I had drunk

Or ~~thrown up all over your carpet~~ emptied some dull opiate to the drains

Alright, officer ~~I'll come quietly~~

2. Longfellow

by the shore of Gitche Gumee
by the shining Big Sea Water
~~by the iggy Piggy Buba~~
~~iggy diggy iggy poo~~
Stood the wigwam of Nakomis
Daughter of the moon Nakomis

3. Tennyson

splendour ~~crads~~ castle / talls
The ~~fishy man sat~~ on ~~the~~ walls
And snowy summits old with story
^ Play~~ing with his willy~~
The light across the l
~~With such a long/shake his trouser snakes~~
And the long cataract leaps in glory
~~Was getting rather chilly~~
Blow ~~you buggers~~, blow, ~~stop the thing from freezing~~ le et wild echoes ly
Blow ~~yourself, the actress said, teasing, teasing, teasing.~~ bugle answer echoes dy dy dy

If I should die
Mary had a little lamb
Think only this of me
And it was always gruntin
There is a corner of some foreign field
She tied it to a five bar gate
That is forever England
And kicked its little XXXX in

T. S. Eliot
4. Ezra Pound

5. Rupert Brooke

6. Percy Bysshe Shelley

K-K-Katy, B-B Beautiful Katy
Let us go then, you and I,
Your the only girl that I adore, when the m,m,moon shines
When the evening is spread out against the sky
On the C, Cow shed
Like a patient etherised upon a table;
I'll be waiting at the k-k-k-kitchen door

weep no more
It was a stinking pool
For Adonais is not dead
And the bugger owed me
such though he be.
A fiver and stinking
Beneath the watery shore
Drowned before he paid me back

7. Shakespere

The quality of mercy is not strain'd
Eeni-meeni-miney-mo
It droppeth as the gentle rain from heaven
Catch a nigger by his toe

William Shakspere

HEY, GANG!

page 71

★ COMING ★

SOON

My GARDEN
by Mr Herbert Thompson

Published in the *Ladies Union Gazette* and the *Siroptomists Newsletter*, May 1954. The author is indebted to the *Psychic Weekly* for the return of his manuscript.

My garden is like a poem
Only full of flowers not words
Instead of rhyme, there's parsley and thyme
And instead of scansion there's birds.

Instead of metre, there's something neater
i.e. rows of pretty things.
Instead of vowels there are spades and trowels
And the sound of the lawn edger sings.

My garden has a compost heap
And herbaceous borders as well.
And where a poem has a thought
My garden has a smell.

My poems are rather like a garden
Only minus the flowers and birds.
And minus the trees and minus the bees
And instead of the plants – there's words.

A puzzle

instructions: cut out the shapes and re-arrange them to form a well-known member of the Royal Family

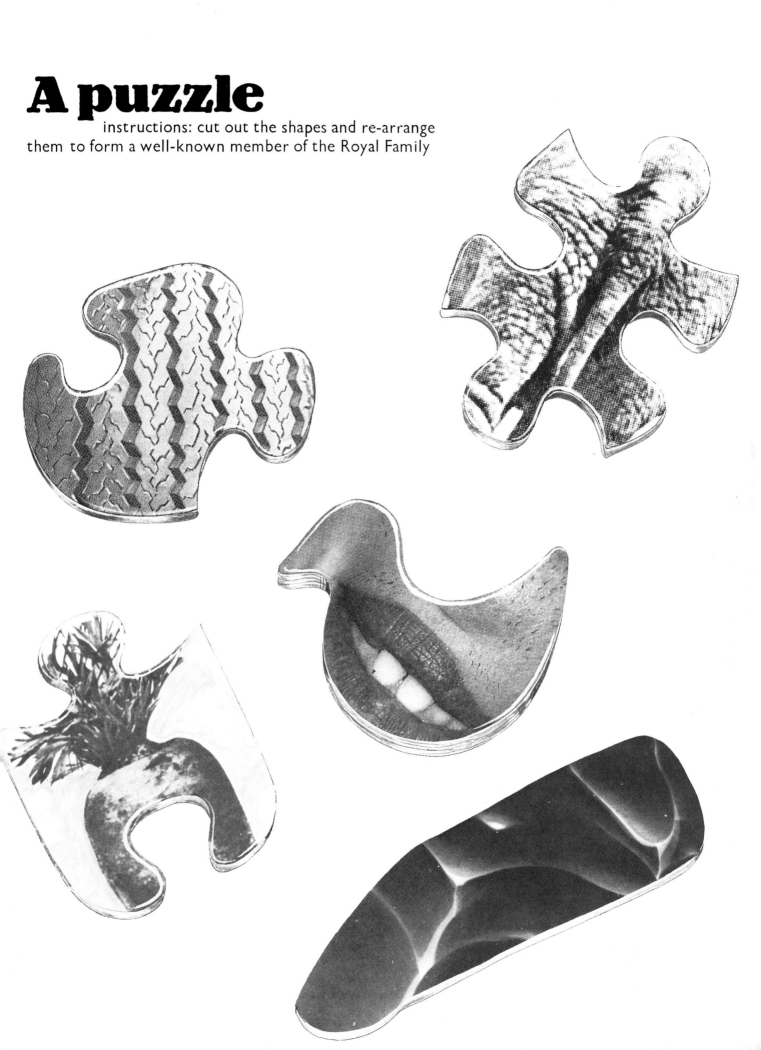

THE BIGOT

'Any Answers'
Hitler
Surrey

Deep down, let's face it, all of us hate foreigners. It's quite
natural when one lives in such a beautiful and perfect country as
our own to hate and loathe those greasy-haired snivelling toadies
from Europe and beyond. What worries me is that sometimes this hat-
red is so deep down that many of us forget about it, and instead of
hitting Frenchmen and letting Dagos' tyres down, we are buying
garlic-smelling French cars and eating filthy chunks of Wop dough in
stinking Pizza parlours. Now I'm not saying that we should go out
and burn down the nearest Eye-tie, Chink, Froggie or Pakki restaurant - I think the army should be doing that - but if we are going
to keep this lovely country of ours beautiful, clean and deeply
religious, we must remember that the Young Bigots Club is only a
phone call away. They will come round at a moment's notice and
tread on packets of Gauloises and throw Grundig equipment down the
lavatory. Remember, Tolerance is a great British virtue - let's
not waste it on Yids, Polacks, Wops, Krauts and Arabs.
Col. Sir Harry McWhirter M.C.C.,
Chairman The Bloody Bigots Club 1937-93

News from our branches:
ASCOT: a very successful Young Bigots' Evening was held in the back
room of the Duck and Prime Minister. A letter of abuse was sent to
M. Pompidou, and a local hairdresser was burned.
The CHELTENHAM branch of the Young Wives' Prejudice Club had a very
successful outing to the Knorr-Swiss Factory. They did over £4,000-
worth of damage.
ESHER Town Hall was packed last Thursday for an illustrated talk by
our local organiser, Mrs. Ursula Fforbes-Hhitler on 'Putting the
Boot in on Wops', and our FRINTON branch have collected over 6,000
dead dogs for our Bulgarian Food Hampers. Well done.

HOLIDAYS
If you must go to the continent, here are some of the places to
visit:
The British Embassy, 35 rue du Faubourg St. Honore, PARIS 8e
The British Embassy, Friedrich Ebert Allee 77, BONN
The British Embassy, Via Conte Rosso 25, ROME
The British Consulate, Herengracht 460, AMSTERDAM
The British Chamber of Commerce, Mesrytiyet Caddessi No.34, Tepbasi
Beyoghi, ISTANBUL

Some useful terms of abuse to help you get the worst out of the
countries you visit:
ITALIANS etc: Greaseballs. Dagos. Wops. Candles. Spaghetti-eaters.
  Ice-cream salesmen. Eye-ties.
EGYPTIANS: Gippos. Yellowbellies. Anti-yids. Sphinctas.
FRENCH: Froggies. Bloody French. (N.B. The French are very
  easily insulted by the British. Almost anything will do.)
GERMANS: Krauts Boche. Sausage-eaters. Square-heads. (N.B.
  The Germans are an appallingly insensitive nation and therefore
  extremely hard to insult. Try setting fire to them or calling
  their Mercedes Volkswagens.)
COLOURED PEOPLE: Best not to even talk to them.

THE LONDON CASEBOOK OF DETECTIVE RENÉ DESCARTES

Chapter 1

The acrid scent of stale cigarette smoke hung wearily in the air of the dingy Whitehall office. The only sound was the querulous buzz of a prying bluebottle indolently hopping among the familiar dun box files clustered above the fireplace occupied by the regulation Scotland Yard electric fire, one bar of which flickered hesitantly in a perfunctory attempt to warm the November gloom.

Detective-Inspector René 'Doubty' Descartes absent-mindedly flicked grey-white ash from the sleeve of his only vicuña jacket and stared moodily across the pigeon-violated rooftops of Whitehall. 'I muse,' he thought. 'Therefore. . . .'

The ginger telephone shrilled its urgent demand. Descartes, rudely awakened from his reverie snatched the receiver to his ear.

'Descartes here,' he posited.

'Sorry to interrupt, sir.' The familiar tones of Sergeant Warnock floated down the line. 'Sergeant Warnock here.'

'How can you be sure?'

'I think I am Sergeant Warnock, therefore I am Sergeant Warnock,' replied Sergeant Warnock confidently. Some of Doubty's thinking was beginning to rub off.

'But if you thought you were Marcus Aurelius would you therefore be Marcus Aurelius?' parried the forensic savant deftly.

'Er . . . probably not,' admitted the trusty sergeant, chancing his arm. When the Detective-Inspector was in moods like this, routine business could take days.

'So, simply because you think you are Sergeant Warnock, it does not necessarily follow that you are,' his postulate continued.

'But, sir, you said, "You think something therefore you are something".'

'No, no, sergeant, you haven't got it at all.'

'Well, sir,' the stalwart sergeant gamely countered, 'there must be a strong probability that I am Sergeant Warnock. Couldn't we on this occasion proceed on that assumption.'

'I'm afraid that it is this "beyond all reasonable doubt" philosophy that has bedevilled the reputation of police thinking since the days of that woolly pragmatist Peel.'

'But this is an urgent matter, sir. The Prime Minister is on the other line.'

'My dear putative sergeant, this problem of your identity, is something we are going to have to sort out sooner or later.'

'But it's the *Prime Minister*, sir.'

'But how do we *know* that it is the Prime Minister?'

'Oh Christ.'

'This is a perfect illustration of my theme, Warnock . . .'

'Aha!'

'. . . if that is indeed to whom I am speaking. If I cannot be sure of the Warnockness of the person or apparent person with whom I am at present speaking, how *a fortiori* can I accept an authentication from this source of a third party of whom my direct and verifiable experience is even further removed?'

'He's rung off anyway, sir.'

'If indeed he was ever there.'

'Well if he was, sir, then he almost definitely asked you to call him back. Can I get him for you, sir?'

'Not so fast, sergeant, for I will assume for the moment that that is who you are.'

'Thank you very much, sir.'

'If I now call the Prime Minister, how is he for certain to know that he is speaking to *me*?'

'Ah but that's *his* problem, sir.'

'But how shall I know that *I* am speaking to *him*?'

'You're calling him, sir.'

'But suppose I speak to someone, thinking him to be the Prime Minister when in fact he is not, *then* the Prime Minister will be disclosing what may well be state secrets to another party, believing him to be me.'

'But surely, sir, just because *you're* speaking to a third party it does not follow as a necessary consequence that the P.M. is speaking to anyone at all.'

Descartes sucked thoughtfully at his familiar thumb. '. . . Good work, sergeant. Get him *toute suite*.' Then replacing the receiver he ruefully swung round on the familiar leather trapeze and stared wistfully out of the window. 'Funny old London,' he thought. At least the pouring rain had stopped. Or rather, it certainly seemed there was no entity a, such that 'χ is rainy and pouring' was true when χ was a, but not otherwise.

Chapter 2

The door of number ten shut and he found himself once again in the oddly unpleasant driving sleet and hail to which his fourteen years in London had still not accustomed him. Setting off briskly across the street, dodging the swishing taxis, he hurried towards the warm and beckoning portals of New Scotland Yard. Why was it, he mused, that the Prime Minister always lost his temper with him? How could the P.M. become so agitated about a country whose very existence had never been properly established? Let alone the intentions of its supposed inhabitants to obtain what the Prime Minister had persisted in referring to as 'secrets'. 'Relative secrets' Doubty could have accepted subject only to a few minor qualifications but his attempts to point out this terminological slackness had received alarming rebuffs from the Prime Minister, a man at the best of times inclined to leap to unsatisfactorily substantiated conclusions, but on this occasion made positively foolhardy by the presence of a man he clearly believed to be the President of the United States of America, on no better evidence, as far as Doubty could deduce, than an exact but superficial physical resemblance to the man normally referred to by the American people as the President, the presence of a couple of hundred alleged 'bodyguards', a so-called Vice-President and a small cavalcade. The last three items, as he had dutifully pointed out, could have been easily faked by a reasonably competent organiser and were in no way contingent upon the Presidentness of the Nixon-like person, while the appearance of the latter, although at first sight impressive to the untrained mind, was still explicable in terms of a twin, a 'double', a highly sophisticated working model, an ordinary optical illusion occurring simultaneously to the apparent Prime Minister and himself, a hallucination caused by the possible presence of certain substances in the Downing Street tea, or, and this was the possibility that Doubty had found increasingly attractive, an oleograph. And it was after all in an attempt to discount this last suspicion that he had struck the putative oleograph the light blow across the top of the head that had caused all the trouble. But why, mused a curious Doubty as he absent-mindedly picked slivers of Prime Ministerial telephone from his scalp, should he now be sent to Tonga in the guise of an ordinary police constable and for an unspecified length of time?

Was *this* to be the Big One?

Chapter 3

The acrid scent of stale coconut milk hung wearily in the air of the sun-drenched Tongan beach. The only sound was the insistent lapping of the prying waves indolently hopping among the familiar dun rock piles clustered about the bay occupied by the regulation Tongan Govern-

THE LONDON CASEBOOK OF DETECTIVE RENÉ DESCARTES

ment-issue catamaran, one float of which glistened hesitantly in a perfunctory attempt to out-shine the August glare. Police Constable René 'Doubty' Descartes absent-mindedly flicked the familiar coconut shells from the sleeve of his only vicuña swimming trunks and stared pointlessly across the crab-befouled beaches of Whitebay. 'I stare pointlessly,' he thought, 'therefore I....' But his reverie was rudely interrupted by the sharp gurgle of a passing flying fish and turning on his familiar heel he picked his way briskly through the swirling lobsters towards the beckoning head of the beach and the equally beckoning cool of the familiar majestic New Reichenbach Falls so many feet above his head and slightly to one side.

As he mounted the ginger path leading to the bridge which so precariously straddled the churning, tumultuous uproar of this watery object, he mentally summarised the past fourteen months.

'Not much, really,' he opined to himself, 'Very little paperwork; very little paper; none at all actually; which is why I am summarizing my thoughts mentally'. Pleased with this conclusion he strode perfunctorily through the driving sunshine past the enchanting pink-shuttered office of the cheery waterfall-keeper, hardly noticing the cluster of blazing bouganvillea just beyond, that reminds one so strongly of the cluster of blazing bouganvillea that one sees just outside Harry's bar, at the corner of Victoria Street and A.A. Milne Crescent, in the main square of Tonga's sleepy capital Tongatapu, where I have been, as you can tell from this description.

By now P.C. Descartes had cautiously stepped out on to the unfamiliar wildly swaying bakelite footbridge which alone stood between him and a watery grave with some bits of rock in it. Staring down into the frothy cascading vortex he nonchalantly flicked the familiar ice-cold spume from his navy-blue vicuña helmet. 'I muse,' he mused, 'therefore I am about to be interrup –'

But his muse was interrupted by the lisping bark he had somehow half-expected.

'Good morning.' Edward de Bono, his arch enemy, and notoriously lateral thinker stood on the bridge, in a mysterious sideways position. 'Good morning,' he rasped angrily. No response . . . 'Good morning,' he re-rasped fiercely, mentally sidling a little. The bakelite bridge seemed to rattle the more violently in reply. Descartes stood his bakelite and mused on the awesome de Bono's existence with all the power he could muster. De Bono, seeing the familiar tell-tale beads of sweat stand out on Doubty's forehead sensed victory. 'Snap!' the bakelite seemed to muse, and a second later, moving laterally, sent the two combatants in an unexpected direction and a probably watery grave respectively.

'A long way down,' the inspector commented inwardly, disbelieving de Bono's existence to the last as he apparently plummeted.

'Somewhere in the distance one could hear the faint familiar cry of an eloping litter-bin,' yelled de Bono, thinking laterally to the last. There was a sickening crash, followed by a sickening cry, then two sickening splashes, a sickening crunch and then three sickening noises that are very difficult to describe.

'So . . . I am dead,' thought Doubty. 'Wait a minute . . . I'm thinking . . . I think, therefore I . . .'

With one logical bound he was.

Chapter 4

The ·22 calibre slug sneaked a lean furrow across the high-gloss teak veneer of the elegant late 1790's Louis XIV dining-table that Madame Capoulet, wife of the Lima Chargé d'Affaires, had had installed at some expense by Serge of Paris the September before last, and thudded into the antique lead Aspidistra stand that propped up the lush flower-strewn wallpaper of the Hardy Fontainebleu Range, straight from the design board of Richard Villon, doyen of the Wallpaper Circle and close friend of Madame Capoulet, who now stood, eyes dilated, nostrils flared in the proud outrage of the French Aristocracy that she had learnt as a small child in the elegant salon of her mother, the Comtesse de St Egrement, all those years ago in the Paris that no longer was,

3

where the chic set gathered on winter mornings and discussed last night's play, sipping English tea, amidst the fine taste and exquisite *décor* of the Boulevard St Michel first-floor flat, with its striped Regency paper, so reminiscent of the Regent Line which is available at Sandersons. Madame Capoulet's neat Dior lipsticked mouth curled into a contemptuous smile as the five-foot-six youth, with his mop of tousled black hair, struggled with the second chamber of his supposedly self-repeating Mauser automatic. She felt strangely sorry for his ill-bred nervousness, as he stood at the open door, and she could look over his grimy-shirted shoulder into the cool hallway beyond, which she had had decorated only last week with that delicate pastel green paper that reminded her so of summer evenings under the trees of the Bois de Boulogne. It was a glorious vindication of the wallpaper designer's art: a discreet, yet striking, combination of jade and malachite, tinted with etiolin shades around the delicately figured tracery of the viridescent flowering cherries that formed the main pattern.

How unlike the paper her late husband had chosen for his bedroom, which was a more modern expression of the time-honoured theme of seasonal contrasts, so beloved of wallpaper designers through the ages. The main design being distinguished by large ovals of umber, oyster and charcoal on the one hand and warm crocus and buttercups on the other, with the intermediary patterns of sepia and ochre interwoven in the fluid shapes of a transient mode.

In the bathroom they had Crown vinyl wallpaper, with a nautical theme of anchors and ships of the line.

The dining-room wallpaper was an original William Morris design, but picked out in modern colours, a simple floral design gives a feeling of space and yet retains the intrinsic feeling of intimacy at £1.90 per yard:

A slightly more daring note is struck with this bold, yet expressive pattern by 'Moderne' of Chelsea, an exclusive luxury class wallpaper

designed to look as if it were worn-out the day it
is put up. An amusing novelty at £6.50 per foot:

In the cheaper range, the 'Evergreens' motif is
always popular – as is the price: £0.15:

Or, if you're feeling really bold, how about
'St Valentine's Day Massacre' at £78 per
centimeter:

ST. VALENTINE'S DAY MASSACRE

BO 0587

American Made

Full Bleed Trim

£4 per roll plus £5 VAT ea.

Hang horizontally

16

APRIL 16 p

ARTICLES

IMPERIAL CHEMICALS AND YOU.
INTERNAL PROTECTION AND DAVID CASSIDY.

EROGENOUS ZONES AND HOW TO AVOID THEM.

AN INTERVIEW WITH MARC BOLAN

FEATURES

ARE YOU USING ENOUGH DEODORANT? BY PETER FIDDICK

Be a 140 wpm sectry & hv sx wth th bss (ADVERT FEATURE)

PLUS:
A FAB INTERVIEW WITH A SURREY CHEMIST. RAYMOND BAXTER LOOKS AT THE NEW DEODORANTS

JAMES BURKE TESTS THE LATEST NON-WASHABLE DEODORANTS

AND

ANOTHER INTERVIEW WITH MARC BOLAN

SHORT STORY

THE DEODORANT By Constance Mac Pseudonym

GRAND COMPETITION

WIN A THOUSAND DEODORANTS and three new Erogenous Zones!

Sixteen. Printed & Published by Amalgamated Chemicals Group. Books, Magazines, Medicaments, Property Development, etc.

EDITORIAL

It's great to be a girl! Yessir it's good to be alive and really feminine in today's world of startling discoveries. Just look what modern science has given the young girl of today: internal tampons, vaginal deodorants, beauty aids so you needn't look ugly, personal body fresheners so you needn't smell, slimming pills so you needn't be fat, diet sheets to help you if you are, underarm deodorants to stop you smelling all day, feet cleansers, hair cleaners, the pill, Marc Bolan and the W.R.A.C.

It's certainly up to you girls to do your best with so much going for you. Now you can be cleaner than any woman in history, and you need never be ashamed or frightened that your body is going to smell, providing you continually use the right medicaments. Of course the moaning minnies are claiming that many of these products are harmful and cause skin damage, but then they would, wouldn't they. So just you get round to the shops and spend, spend, spend.　　　Vera

DEAR SISSIE.

Dear Caroline,
I suspect you are either using the wrong tampon, or the wrong type of toothpaste, or you're too fat. Try changing your deodorant for more intimate freshness, and washing your hair in stronger lotion. Are you sure that you are quite fresh in those delicate areas all girls have? Smudgies have a new product out called 'Personal' which squirts on those difficult places.

Dear Susan,
No of course you don't stink all over. I wish I knew where you girls get these ideas.
*　　　Yours, SISSIE*
P.S. Have you tried the new feet cleanser by Samules, price 40p? Its great.

Dear Connie,
No of course you can't get pregnant like that. It's purely for intimate freshness only.

Dear Alice,
I would strongly recommend that you change your deodorant, but don't go to the Police; Chemical Firms are only human. Human tissue can easily be replaced nowadays, and it's better than smelling, isn't it.
*　　　Regards, SISSIE*

Dear SISSIE,
I AM SIXTEEN AND WORRIED. HOW CAN I SPEND MORE ON INTIMATE FRESHNESS? Sally-Anne.
Join the WRAC. It's a grand life and you get an allowance.

15-year-old Annie (name and address supplied on request) has written in to ask which vaginal deodorant Cliff Richard uses. Well we phoned and asked him personally but he was out.
Incidentally Slater-Chemicals are giving away a year's free supply to any girl who can come up with a new area that needs deodorizing. All you have to do is describe the area in not more than your own words and then say why you think it smells. P.S. This competition is not open to employees of Slater-Chemicals or Solicitors (or scientists).

RECORD REVIEWS

'Honey you smell' sings Butch on his latest LP 'Feelings'. One knows what he means. Great to hear Flab back in form with their new waxing 'Internal Protection During the Difficult Time'. Salem records are giving away deodorants with their new singles. Great idea.

NEXTWEEK

Janet comes across the mysterious Mr Feldman.
Plus: An interview with Marc Bolan.
Also: Another interview with Marc Bolan.
Soon: Special attraction: three interviews with Marc Bolan. What is he *really* like?

Your Guide To SLIMMING

By a Harley Street Nutritionist
Good evening. I am a Harley Street nutritionist. My address is 42b, Harley St., Slough. A lot of people mock when I say: 'Harley St., Slough', but it doesn't make a ha'porth of difference to my professional standing just because I live in Harley Street, Slough. I have outstanding qualifications as a nutritionist which apply whether I live in Slough or Salzburg – I am a fully-fledged D.A.N. (Mans.). (A Doctor of Applied Nutritionism (Mans.).) A lot of people mock when I say that I have a degree from Mans but there is no need to mock – I don't care if Auden or Isherwood or Bertrand Russell didn't go to Mans – it makes not a scrap of difference to me. So let's stop knocking nutritionists just because they don't come from the Harley Street we all know, where the rents are so bloody high that only international abortionists and Bobby Darin's plastic surgeon can ever afford even space for a couch – let alone a toilet and . . . I'm sorry. Anyway, let's get down to the Slimming Course I have devised. It's called the *Harley Weight-Reducing Course,* and is designed to make you slimmer almost overnight, whilst actually eating and drinking far, far more.

How Does It Work?
Well, as we all know, Fat is caused by the movement of the Moon in conjunction with the planets of our solar – what are you laughing at? What are you laughing at, Mr Oxford-educated Harley Street Specialist? Fancy yourself as a nutritionist, eh? Oh! Let's all have a good laugh at the nutritionist from Mans, eh? Well, if you weren't so fat and flabby and ugly and . . . I'm sorry. Here's my Ideal Daily Diet:

Harley Weight-Reducing Diet
(Suggested Daily Menu)
Breakfast:
2 platefuls of jelly
1 lump of dough
a melon
3 kippers
fried egg and self-raising flour
6 cups of tea
toast and marmalade
more lumps of dough
bread and butter
3 pints of cream
another melon

Lunch:
1 tub lard
3 lbs sausages
2 large meringues
lemon tea (no sugar)

Supper:
Salmon mousse
Quiche Lorraine
Treacle Tart
Chips
Bread
Lard
Chocolate
Dough
Beer
Animal fat
Cream
Butter
Pastry
Sugar
Plastic sheeting
Tin
Copper
Lead
Steel
Helium
Coffee (*black – no sugar*)
By the end of the first day you should have lost 24 lb.

What People Have Said About The Harley Weight-Reducing Course:
'A complete fraud' Mrs D'A., Cheltenham
'Painful and extremely fattening' M.B. of Deptford
'A waste of time and money' D. La Pouge, Naples
'Wonderful. Couldn't be improved upon'. Dr. A., Harley Street (Slough)
'The Ascent of F6' Auden and Isherwood (Mans)

Summer Madness

Short story by
Elaine Gibson

Tenderly Renaldo took me in his arms and pressed his hot Italian lips into my reluctant Reigate ear.

"Now, now, Chérie," he murmured, his warm body responding roughly to my gentle caresses. But it wasn't Renaldo who occupied my thoughts. My mind and body cried out only for Ron. Ron, Ron, Ron. When I thought of those intimate moments in his dusty darkroom as our relationship developed I could hardly believe the evidence of the photographs I'd found. Had that really been Olga? It was hard to tell on those grainy prints, with her face so far away from camera. But those socks were definitely Ron's. Perhaps I should have given him a chance, faced him with the evidence instead of running for the sun with only the tarnished memory of a shattered love and some WRAC pamphlets in my suitcase. In many ways I was still a schoolgirl.

'Now, now, mon amour,' Renaldo was panting. But my mind was far away. I was dreaming of the playing fields at Maytown School, and those glorious summers when youth blossomed like an oleocanth, and Jack the groundsman from the local pub filled my adolescent dreams with forbidden desires. Many a time we'd run to the secret place at the back of the Science Lab., dreaming love's dreams and melting into a thousand embraces.

"Now, now, I beg you," Renaldo pleaded, his hot brown body locked against mine in the warm shade of sunny Spain. But my mind was far away from the pizzas, plane trees, and zabaglione of the Costa del Sol. I was dreaming of Mr Robinson my first maths master, and how he'd taught me all he knew and showed me something wonderful: the rosy path of love. I yearned to be there now, in that crazy ramshackle little shed of his, far away from the false values of fourteen days of fun with the inevitable return to

---

The story so far: For the past seventeen weeks Janet has been on a fantastic package tour to Malaga trying to forget Ron, tall blonde photographer's assistant, whom she thinks is having an affair with Olga, her vivacious Russian flatmate. On the beach at Torremolinos (Spain) summer romance has caught up with her in the shape of Renaldo, a hairy wop waiter from the local café. Beguiled by her English freshness, Renaldo has asked her to spend the night with him on some rush matting behind the Spanish National Tourist Office, but she can't help thinking of Ron and wondering where he is. . Now read on.

---

the reality of Luton airport. This was only a fleeting affair, just a holiday romance. Oh, when would I grow up?

'Now, now,' Renaldo shouted but my mind was far away, thinking that this too would all too quickly end and I should return to the flat in Gloucester Road, and the problems of working as a Temp for Mr Bigglesworth, the famous film producer. Why would he never look at me? Why would he never speak to me? Who was the mysterious Giles who was always with him? Why did *he* never look at me? Was it something to do with me?

"Now, now," Renaldo screamed, his hot body furiously close, but my mind was miles away. A million miles away in San Francisco, L.A., where Tony the drummer had gone with "The Maybe". He told me he'd write, perhaps he was too busy being successful to remember a little secretary like me. I thought of the intimate atmosphere of his dressing-room in those five minutes when we'd met backstage. I tried to think of his face, but could only remember his belt, and that crazy zip.

"Oh damn," said Renaldo. "Look, you wait here I'll have to go and clean up." But I hardly heard him. My mind was far away, dreaming of Bobby the dress-designer and wondering whether he would ever return from Hamburg. . . .

To be continued

PYTHON PANEL *A candid conversation*

PANELISTS

RUTH FRAMPTON: *Britain's first woman judge and a leading exponent of Women's Lib.*

VICE-POPE ERIC: *the No. 2 man in the Vatican.*

BRIAN STALIN, *eldest brother of the USSR's late great Dictator.*

DR EDWARD KRASZT: *American sociologist and author of* All Anyone Need Know About Anything.

PYTHON: Good Evening.

ALL EXCEPT KRASZT: Good Evening.

KRASZT: I didn't say 'Good Evening' then because I wanted a line to myself.

PYTHON: We take your point, Dr Kraszt. Vice-Pope Eric?

VICE-POPE: Not at the moment, thank you.

PYTHON: Brian?

STALIN: I'm fine thanks. How about Miss Frampton?

PYTHON: Well we are going to ask her our first question so that's not really necessary.

ALL: Fine.

PYTHON: Ruth Frampton, in 1959 you became the first woman to be made a judge of Quarter Sessions in this country.

FRAMPTON: *My* first line is just to say 'That's right'.

PYTHON: Why do you claim to be Sir Edmund Hillary's mother?

STALIN: What? I've never said I . . .

PYTHON: No, we were talking to Miss Frampton.

STALIN: Sorry, I thought you were looking at me.

KRASZT: It's a bit confusing you know.

PYTHON: Shut up please. (LAUGHTER)

KRASZT: I didn't hear anyone laugh.

PYTHON: To return to our question. Why do you claim a maternal situation vis-à-vis the first conqueror of Everest?

FRAMPTON: Because I *am* his Mum. He is my little Edmund, bless his little pitons, and he has been a wonderful boy to me.

PYTHON: But Sir Edmund has it on record that he knows his mother well and that she and you are definitely separate persons.

FRAMPTON: Then he is being naughty because he is over-tired. All boys are naughty sometimes; to expect them to be perfect is quintessentially daft.

PYTHON: Dr Kraszt?

KRASZT: This is probably correct. The recent survey of 420,000 people, carried out at Michigan University over a period of eight years by Professors Rinehart, Schwartz, Zincstein and Semite, indicates conclusively that people – not just boys, interestingly enough – are by and large not absolutely perfect. A statistically significant proportion of them, at some stage in the 70-odd-years maturation process, do something they ought not to really. These findings constitute something of a breakthrough in this field.

PYTHON: Thank you Dr Kraszt.

FRAMPTON: You see? So I am *definitely* his mother.

PYTHON: But were you actually present at his birth?

FRAMPTON: No. I can't claim that. At the time I was unavoidably detained at the Hague, where I had the honour to represent my country in the International Legal Championships. Edmund knows it was impossible for me to be there and has never held it against me.

STALIN: Then why is he applying for an injunction against the publication of your forthcoming book?

FRAMPTON: Because, Brian, I reveal in *My Son, the Clambering Knight* that before the final assault, he tied a large weight to Tensing so that he could get to the top first.

STALIN: Tensing's mother has confirmed this story to me. The weight, incidentally, is now in the Tensing Family Museum on K2 along with other Sherpa-connected objects.

FRAMPTON: Anyway Eddie is excrementally scared that when this gets out they will confiscate his knighthood, which would cost him a few bob in directorships. Even so, I think he has overreacted.

KRASZT: This can happen of course. People do sometimes overreact to things – that is to say, when things happen, these people – in fact, all of us – occasionally react over-wise, as it were, to these very things. To put it another way, a perfectly ordinary stimulus produces an overreaction, O. This has been shown time and time again in studies undertaken by the Californian Institute for Making Studies under Luxurious Conditions.

FRAMPTON: Exactly. Anyway Eddie is a Kiwi poppet; it is this woman who happened to be around when he came to light who is playing dog in the manger.

PYTHON: To change the subject, how about sex?

FRAMPTON: Sex is a fine and wonderful gift *provided* that it is accompanied by a feeling of love and involvement for whoever it is you happen to be banging away with at the time.

PENTHOUSE: How about pubic hair?

PYTHON: Come out from behind those curtains! Now go away and take your ludicrous catchphrases with you.

PENTHOUSE: Sorry. (EXEUNT)

PYTHON: So a feeling of love and involvement is necessary?

FRAMPTON: Or at least a reasonable pretence at it.

KRASZT: I think it's important to distinguish between premarital sex, that is sex before marriage; extra-marital sex, that is sex outside a marriage, or extra sex within; pseudo-marital sex, which is marital sex where the marriage is invalid due to an oversight in the ceremony or mistaken identity; ultra-marital sex, which is sex over and above the marital sex; quasi-marital sex where the two partners, being married, believe themselves to be making love when in fact they are not; post-marital sex which is sex after the marriage *or* after the divorce; and amarital sex, which is sheer simple-minded, out-of-context banging. Then there is pre-sexual marriage where the spouses are unusually timid, busy or maladroit; extra-sexual marriage wh . . .

PYTHON: Vice-Pope Eric? What is the Catholic position?

VICE-POPE: Well I've never personally, er . . . so I wouldn't . . .

PYTHON: No, no, on sex and marriage.

VICE-POPE: Oh. Well our main worry at this stage is intra-marital sex.

PYTHON: Oh. Sex *within* the marriage.

KRASZT: I missed that.

VICE-POPE: Oh yes! You see, it's *within* marriage, people tend to forget, that most of this carnal knowing takes place.

PYTHON: But *that* isn't wrong from a Catholic point of view?

VICE-POPE: Well, actually . . . it is. Yes. I mean we don't often come straight out with it because our problem is that . . . like it or not, sex, at this moment in time, is still the best method we've got of reproducing ourselves. I mean we certainly recommend virgin births where possible, but we can't rely on them, so for purely practical reasons we've been forced to turn a blind eye to intra-marital sex *for the time being*. But only of course for outnumbering purposes; not for *fun*.

KRASZT: Which is why you will not allow

any form of contraception.

VICE-POPE: Exactly.

FRAMPTON: But you allow the rhythm method!

VICE-POPE: Ah, but only because it doesn't work.

PYTHON: But are you not worried that the population explosion may lead to greater poverty, disease and eventually war?

VICE-POPE: Well you must remember, our concern is for the next world. So the quicker we can get people there the better.

FRAMPTON: Your vice-holiness, can you advise me how I should tell Eddie about sex. Whenever I try to bring the subject up casually, he becomes embarrassed.

VICE-POPE: Well, frankly, it's not easy. I mean, take the sex act. Please. (LAUGHTER) Well, none of us can work out what God must have been thinking of when He dreamed it up. I mean . . . you know what these people actually do, do you? It's a mind-boggler isn't it! Going to the lavatory is bad enough but . . .

KRASZT: That's not a sin though.

VICE-POPE: Only if indulged in to excess. Voluntarily that is. *Bona fide* diarrhoea is morally impeccable, but, if deliberately self-induced, can be a venial one.

PYTHON: To return to sex. (CHEERING)

STALIN: What about Communism?

PYTHON: Later, later. Vice-Pope, did Christ himself say anything about sex being sinful?

VICE-POPE: Apparently not, no. This was obviously an oversight on his part, which fortunately we have been able to rectify, with the help of the teachings of Paul . . .

PYTHON: The Pope?

VICE-POPE: No, no, the saint. The woman-hater.

PYTHON: Oh, the pouf.

VICE-POPE: So they say, yes. Anyway, we've managed to pass this off as Christ's teaching, rather successfully as I think you will admit.

ALL: Absolutely. First class job.

FRAMPTON: Had me fooled.

VICE-POPE: So that even where sex has been . . . well, permitted, the guilt's been in there, doing its job.

FRAMPTON: Does this necessity to sub-edit Christ sometimes worry you?

VICE-POPE: Not really. After all, you can't treat the New Testament as gospel. And one must remember that Christ, though he was a fine young man with some damn good ideas, did go off the rails now and again, rich-man-eye-of-camel for example, which is only to be expected, because he came from a difficult background . . . an under-privileged Jewish family, his father, God, God the Father that is, was all over the place, in addition to which He wasn't married to Christ's mother . . .

FRAMPTON: But Joseph was.

VICE-POPE: Yes, but Mary was a virgin you see, so the marriage could never have been consummated and so was not legally valid.

PYTHON: So, either way, Christ was a bit of a bastard?

VICE-POPE: Yes, an almighty bastard of course but . . . This sort of thing helps to explain, too, why he became polygamous in his after-life; all nuns being brides of Christ, as you know.

KRASZT: But with certain exceptions, you accept his teaching?

VICE-POPE: Oh yes, it's been an invaluable basis for our whole operation really. Of course people accuse us sometimes of not practising what we preach, but you must remember that if you're trying to propagate a creed of poverty, gentleness and tolerance, you need a very rich, powerful, authoritarian organisation to do it.

FRAMPTON: I'm afraid I must go now. I have to get Eddie's tea ready.

PYTHON: Well we've almost finished. Could you just hold on till we get to the bottom of the page.

STALIN: What? You mean we have to finish there?

PYTHON: Yes. The next page is full of some very good drawings.

STALIN: But I want to tell you about being Joe Stalin's elder brother. What it felt like to grow up in a family where a tiny child was organising purges the whole time! The knock at the nursery door in the middle of the night, the way Joe got rid of Dad and had Auntie Vanya installed as a puppet-father, how he got our smallest sister, Catherina, made eldest brother by giving the dog an extra vote! How can I tell all that in seven lines?

PYTHON: Six

STALIN: Well I soon realised the way things were going after all the shooting at Boris's Christening, so I packed my worldly goods and with jaunty step set off for the legendary city of Dundee, in Scotland

PYTHON: Sorry. That's it

STALIN: Can't I go on down here?

PYTHON: No. It doesn't look nice.

RUTH FRAMPTON

VICE-POPE ERIC

BRIAN STALIN

DR EDWARD KRASZT

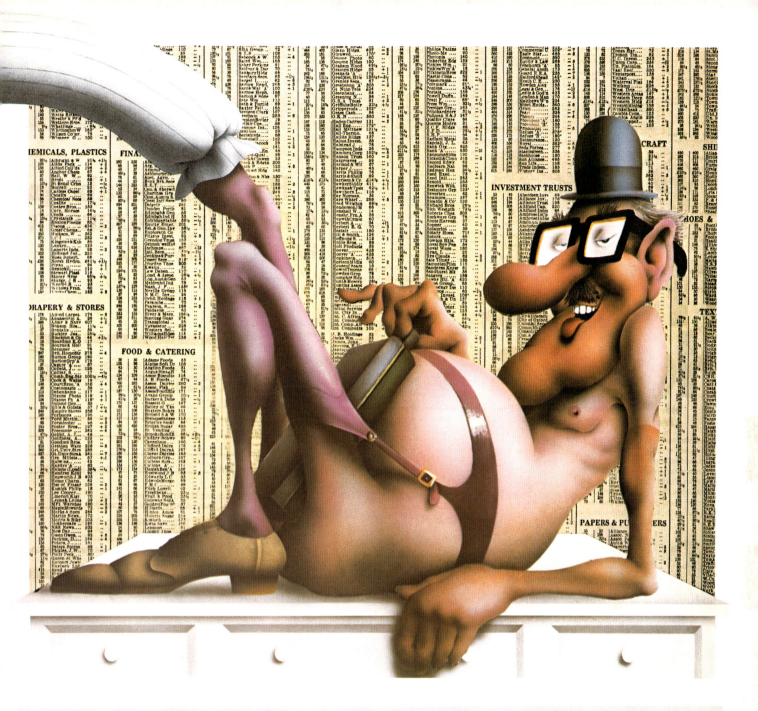

Mr April

I've got two legs
from my hips to the ground
And when I move them
they walk around

And when I lift them
they climb the stairs
And when I shave them
they ain't got hairs.

T	W	T	F	S	S	M	T	W	T	F	S	S	M	T
1	2	3	4	5	6	7	8	9	10	11	12	13	14	15
W	T	F	S	S	M	T	W	T	F	S	S	M	T	W
16	17	18	19	20	21	22	23	24	25	26	27	28	29	30

Competition Time

Put these six photographs of Richard Nixon in order of merit and YOU can WIN Lulu (or the cash equivalent)* (providing you're over 21)

Don't Wait until the Last Minute

In addition choose three of the following qualities you think most suit R. M. Nixon.

Nixon's the one because he is:

☐ a) sincere
☐ b) handsome
☐ c) ruggedly honest

☐ d) a second-hand car dealer
☐ e) hot on law and order
☐ f) American
☐ g) husband to Pat, and daddy to Tricia

Booby Prize: Complete the couplet and win an extra 1,000 pieces of cutlery.*

I like Tricky Dicky cos ....
....

WIN Free!

* *Guaranteed non-melting*

Competition sponsored by 'Democrats for Fascism' Watergate Buildings

ello and welcome to this page, which as you can see is a most unusual page in that it is laid out quite differently from the usual way in
hich pages in books are laid out, and obviously you are going to be wondering why, especially if you have bothered to strain your eyes by
ading this far. Well, if you are wondering this, then you are obviously a smart fellow. If you are a fellow of course. If you're not a fellow
en you're a smart lady, or whatever, it doesn't really matter in any case. The fact remains that you are smart. Well, then, you are wonder-
g, why this particular layout for this particular page, which doesn't look as though it has anything to offer to the casual reader at first
ance? However, you would be quite wrong to think that it has nothing to offer. You wouldn't be as smart as I at first thought you were if
u thought that. Because, quite simply, this page is in competition with a lot of other pages, in an unusual way. This page is attempting to
at the world record for the number of words printed on any single individual page. How about that? So you are involved in what is an
tempt on a world record, which automatically makes it more exciting than a lot of other pages you've read in this book. In fact I personally
ink this page is the most exciting in the whole book, and if it wins and beats the record then obviously it will stand a chance of being the
ost exciting page ever written in any book in the world. And you will have read it. So how about that? You will have a chance to say
sually in conversation that you have read the most exciting page in the world. Of course people will question you and pooh-pooh you but
u will know that if this world record attempt is successful and if it is ratified by the World Publishing Council and recognized as a world
cord then you will have taken part in it by reading the most exciting page in the world. And what's more it won't have had to rely on cheap
oys to get you excited. It won't have captured your imagination simply by describing exciting events like a tall dark man in a white suit
restling against the curse of four gorillas in a semi-tropical jungle whilst his arch enemy Von Methuen approached with the entire Eighth
rmy bent on his destruction. Oh no, there will be none of that spurious interest that any writer can so easily whip up to keep your imagina-
on ticking over with the illusion that what you are reading is exciting. Neither will there have been any purple passages of fine prose with the
awn lancing across the steamy mud of the paleolithic swamp which lay drenched in the succulent colours of first light type of writing that
ons you into thinking that you are reading some very exciting stuff by a first-rate writer when in fact any chap with O levels and an editor
ho can spell can churn out such prose with the ease of a practised Graham Greene. So you see this page has none of these spurious additions
hich are mistaken for excitement, because it contains *real* tension, rather than imaginary tension, in so far as you have become involved in this
cord-breaking attempt. And together we are steaming towards the bottom of the page, racing for the line there where we shall find out
hether or not we have been successful TOGETHER, and surely it's this kind of togetherness which sets a new first in publishing history. So
y building up real tension you will be sitting on the edge of your seat by the end of this page, absolutely worn out from reading, and yet
xpectant and tense to see whether WE have beaten a WORLD RECORD. Won't it be exciting if we have! Just think of it. THE page in the
tire history of the world that contains the most words on any single page. No book in the whole Universe, so far as we know, will contain
many words. Isn't that exciting? And then there will be all the tension of the many challenges from around the world that will be bound
ensue from a successful win here today. Wow, I can hardly wait, to get to the end of the page. Oh dear I'm tiring a little. Oh heavens.
m starting to feel a little faint. What on earth shall I do? Keep going you fool. Keep it churning out at all costs, why you must be easily
alfway there by now. What a place to break down! Oh gosh I can see the headlines now: British Page Breaks Down Only An Agonising Few
ches From The World Record. Plucky British Page Just Fails In World Record Attempt. And just think of it, some German or dago page
bound to nip into first place. Must keep going. Think of England. Consider the pride of the English Publishers. How great to take home
is triumph, might even be a decoration in it, certainly something for the Chairman of Eyre Methuen I wouldn't wonder. Keep it going,
d, think of home, think of what it means to be British, 'Land of Hope and Glory, Mother of the free', that's it, keep singing, you're nearly
ere, 'How shall we extol thee, Who are borne of thee'. I'm starting to feel much better. 'Wider still and wi-der'. Yes yes. 'Shall thy bounds
spread'. Oh boy. 'God who made thee mighty. Make theee mightier yet'. I'm feeling just great. 'God who ma-de thee mighty. Make thee
ightier yet'. Oh thank God. I feel just dandy. So strong and proud and full of energy and stamina, I feel I could go on and on and con-
nue to win the most words in a single chapter, even the most words in a book. Well perhaps not today. I should save the big one until I've
ained a little. Start with one world record before smashing on to a second. Boy do I feel good! That's patriotism for you. You see what I
ean, just what I was talking about before my little trouble back there? This is what REAL excitement is about. Now we nearly failed there,
gether, you and I, for without me you couldn't have gone racing on to the end of the page and victory all by yourself. No, not even if you
ok a pencil and started filling in the blank bit that I had left, by yourself, because that would have been cheating, and cheats never prosper
d in any case it wouldn't have been ratified by the World Publishing Council because your words wouldn't have been printed words. So you
e we need each other, we're in this race together, dependent on one another in a fine and free relationship between author and reader,
ithout me having to bribe you with any of the usual garbage, such as sex, to keep your mind on the job whilst we race for the edge of the
age. I've never once had to stoop to mentioning any kind of sex you'll be glad to have noticed. I've not had to resort to keeping you enter-
ined with indiscreet glimpses into the bed or bathroom to keep your eyes ploughing that lonely printed furrow. Oh no, sir, and now do you
e how unnecessary page after page of sexy talk and writing is in books. I don't know why authors stoop to putting such things in, surely it's
ly to boost sales, and yet you aren't taken in by such smutty talk are you? To read a book successfully to the end you don't have to be
tillated with little glimpses of Janet's silken thigh as she discreetly drops her peignoir and steps naked on to the bathrug. You don't need to
e her run her fingers carelessly through her long black hair, or watch the fine tanned muscles in her back moving lightly and easily under
e effort. Not for you, surely, the necessity to see her standing under the shower in the fine full nakedness of a young woman of twenty. To
el the splash of the warm water tingling against the firm skin, to watch her hair dampening, and falling in long black coils across her firm
osoms, to feel her nipples becoming firm with the kiss of the shower, her body arching up into the warmth, losing herself in the sensual feel
the water, pushing her thighs towards the tingle of the spray, the damp hair rubbing roughly against the soap in her hands, as she covers her
ody in the sensuous warm glow, and feels her very soul alive with excitement. Only then did she become aware of John's naked body beside
r in the shower. No, this is not for you. Of course not. You don't need such cheap ploys or such shoddy writing to keep you involved in
ading. Not for you a sense of disappointment when the dirty bits end and the quick flicking of pages to see where the next love story begins. You're
t the sort of person to let the library book fall open at the most thumbed pages I can tell, because you have chosen to follow this race through, with
e real excitement of a race rather than the imaginary mental stimulation that the mind so easily picks up from any second rate, cheapskate
ovelette. And look, there's the bottom of the page looming up. We're going to do it. It's going to be our record, I feel sure. We're in the stadium
ow and the crowd is roaring us home. We're going to do it. Keep smiling, this is the moment of victory when we can throw down the pen and
lax into the long warm smile of triumph. This is it lads. Surely we've done it. Now's the time for the champagne, the celebrations
d cheers of the book critics. The world of interviews and press photos and lunch with the editor of the New Statesman is opening
for us. We're at the line. It's ours, We've done it. I'm sure we've finally done (turn to next page for the result) certainly.

The Result of the World record Attempt in the Most Words on a Single Page, Ratified by the World Publishing Council.
The attempt by Page 35 of the Brand New Monty Python Bok has I'm afraid just narrowly been beaten by two words. Had they not printed turn to next page for the result, then they would have been clear winners. Bad luck. And what a brave attempt! So now it's up to Margaret Drabble, or Graham Greene to take up the cudgels on behalf of Great Britain.

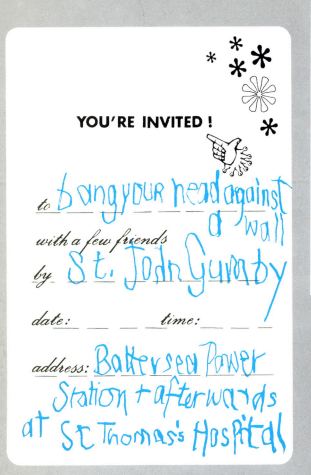

YOU'RE INVITED !

to *bang your head against a wall*

with a few friends

by *St. John Gumby*

date: time:

address: *Battersea Power Station + afterwards at St Thomas's Hospital*

INSTRUCTIONS: Cut out, fill in your name and place one or two of these on your mantel-piece.

Richard, Pat and Tricia

take great personal pleasure
in inviting

....

to a private performance of Christmas Carols,
bombing premitting, on 24th December

at The White House, Washington D.C.
R. S V. P. The State Dept. or any large corporation

DAVID FROST

invites you to
Contribute material to his Shows

R.S.V.P.
'Telejape'

HOWARD HUGHES

requests
The Pleasure of Your Company
on July 8th, at 2.45 a.m.

the third desk along, Delta Airways check-in counter, La Guardia Airport, New York, on receipt of a pink and green hold-all marked with a 'London–Khartoum' Sudan airways label, you will receive a sealed brown envelope. Take this, with no hand luggage please, to the Wills and Securities counter of the National Bank of Montana's Seattle Branch. Leave the brown envelope face downwards on counter and ask for Mr Betty Saward. He will take you to No. 8 platform Seattle Central Station. Wait here for the 9.15 Denver–Houston express. When it comes in, enter the third compartment from the left in the 6th coach and crawl through into the Chicago stopping train alongside. As soon as this leaves crawl out on to the platform and double back into the back of the Denver train, hiding in the mailbag marked K4. Once in Lagos go straight to the Holiday Inn in Nomulu Street and ask for 'Grace' or 'Gracie'. He will introduce you to the Men's Room attendant, who will give you a sealed can of microfilm with the name of the architect of the hotel. He will give you a hat-check ticket for the Colombo Hilton. Collect the hat in the name of Mr Nothingsuspiciousaboutme and inside will be a card marked with the name of a Chinese city. Destroy the card and forget the name. As soon as it gets dark take a northbound flight to Madras, double back to Mysore and take the sleeper to Hyderabad. Leave the station at Hyderabad and turn left, right, left again, right, left, sharp right, bringing your left foot in behind your partner's right, toe pointing outwards, and turn and two and swing and turn and bring the right leg in, turn left again and Howard Hughes is the shoe-black with the green shorts and the beret. Please be punctual.

R.S.V.P.
Howard Hughes,
Third desk along, Victoria
Coach Terminal reserve
bookings counter, ask for
a Mr Cripps, wearing a green

Aristotle & Mrs Onassis

request the pleasure
of

....'s Company

for supper on WEDNESDAY 28th APRIL

Private Jet from Heathrow 5.00
Cocktails 7.00   White Tie

The Australian Wino Society

invite you to

An Australian Wine Tasting

Bring your own bottle   R. S. V. P. Grog House
                                                    Regurgitation St.,
Free Sheilas   Earls Court, S.W.7.

IAN SMITH

invites you to
celebrate the opening of his new chin

7 for 6.30

**Black Tie
No Blacks**

Martin & Mrs Bormann
~~~~~~~~~~~~~~~~~~

Demand the pleasure of your Company
at a Non-Nazi Re-Union Dinner Dance

Black tie   R.S.V.P. The Daily Express
Armbands   Scoop Buildings

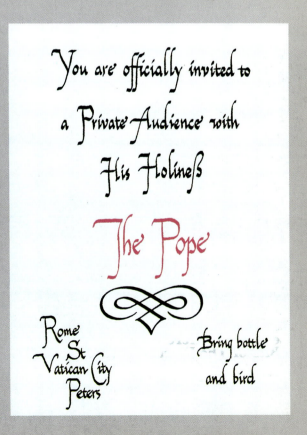

You are officially invited to

a Private Audience with

His Holiness

The Pope

Rome
St
Vatican City
Peters

Bring bottle
and bird

A a
Aard-vark a very difficult word which you don't need to know.
Abacinate another word which is totally useless and you won't ever use, so don't go fretting over it or looking it up in another dictionary because honestly it's pointless
Aback aback
Abacus a very similar word to 'Aback'.
Abalone *see* 'Aard-vark'
Abandon to abandon
Abbey an abbey
Abbot an abbot
Abbreviate to abbreviate
Abdicate to abdicate
Abdication ditto (near enough)
Abditory also similar
Abdomen same again except for 5 letters
Abduct almost the same
Aberration an almost totally different word – ignore it
Abettor abdomen
Abeyance *see* 'Aard-vark'

Knickers ladies' underpants
Abhorrent I wouldn't worry about what this word means
Abide abdicate
Abigail lady's maid
Ability ability
Abject abdicate
Abjure abject (only three letters' difference and they try to pass it off as a different word! Just shows those mealy-mouthed egg-heads in the universities haven't got anything better to do than split hairs over tiny little details that don't make a fart of difference to people's lives. Abject/abjure what's the difference? Who cares anyway?)
Ablative This kind of thing really makes me sick! Does it matter a tinker's cuss what different endings they used to have in a language nobody speaks any more.
Ablaze ablaze
Able able
Abnegate to abjure! (It really is! Look it up in the

O.E.D. if you don't believe me!)
Abnormal abnormal
Aboard aboard
Abode abode
Abolish abolish (this is what dictionaries ought to be like)
Abominable abominable
Abortion abortion
Abound abound
About about
Above above
Abracadabra abracadabra
Hey presto! hey presto!
Shazam! shazam!
Oogie-woogie its a boogie!
Abreast *not* 'a breast'
Abroad practically the same as 'Aboard' – in fact it's just got one tiny weeny little letter in a different place and they try to pass it off as a different word! Therefore, very definitely, *see* 'Aboard'.
Abrupt abrupt
Abscess a collection of pus or purulent matter formed by a morbid process in a cavity of the body. Great!

It's words like that that make a dictionary really worthwhile.
Absolute absolute
Absolution absolute
Absolutist absolute
Absolutory absolute
Absolve absolute
Absonant absolute
Absorb absolute
Abstract abstract
Absurd absurd
Abuse abuse
Abyss abyss
Acadialte oh piss off.

B

Buttock buttock
Bum bum
Tit tit

This is the end of the 'Oxfod' Simplified Dictionary. Words beginning with the letter C onwards are seldom used, and hardly worth including in a genuine simplified dictionary. N.B. We do not *refund money to clever-dicks who want to look up other words. So there. Ed.*

The Oxfod Home University Coarse
(Learn everything you need to know to get a B.A.(Oxfod) in three lessons!)

With only three lessons of the **Oxfod Home University Coarse** you can get a real genuine degree in any of the following subjects:
Ballooning
Botany
Bio-chemistry
Brain-surgery
Chemistry (same as Bio-chemistry)

Coal-mining (practical)
Corks
Danish Literature
French (not as interesting as you'd think. I don't recommend this)
Gemistry (see Bio-chemistry)
High-jump
Interesting Facts
Mathematics (boring)
Pencils

Physics (same as Bio-chemistry)
Geography (should have been with the G's – sorry)
Reading
Rolling Down Grass Banks (one of the best coarses of the lot)
Studying (rotten)
Spy-writing (you'll need to buy a Platignum 'Spy-

Master' invisible pen set for this coarse)
Sums
Tortures
Uther Tortures
Very Nasty Tortures
Wizard Tortures
X-Cert Tortures
Yelling
Zoo (sorry – couldn't think of anything else)

Geography

Here is a specimen coarse:

Lesson 1: The World, A General Geographical Introduction

The World is round. It has seventy-two different countries and they're all on dry land. The rest of the World is in the sea.
Why doesn't the world float? Well, if you go into your garden, and pick up a bit of the world and put it in a jam-jar of water, you'll find that it sinks right down to the bottom, and this practical experiment concludes our first lesson: The World Is Heavier Than You Think.

Lesson 2: Different Bits of The World

China: It's a long way away, so you don't need to know too much about it.

But basically, China is a very small, unimportant country with a large Asian population. It just shows the results of not curbing immigration soon enough. But oh no – nobody wanted to listen to Mr Powell and now look at the way the country's going.
India: This is worse than China, because they're all Pakis with unlimited freedom to walk around – and they don't even have to sign with the police! It's ruined India which used to be quite nice
America: Much more like England. The Queen of America is called the President and at the moment it's a man. In fact America has never had a Queen on the throne, except possibly Warren G. Harding, mainly because American ladies are

not gracious enough. In any case they all have deep-freezers and are very contented. Unlike China, America is extremely large. So large, in fact, that the travelogue I saw only had time to deal with one part, but evidently the most important part: Yellowstone National Park. This is really beautiful, evidently, and you can drive round it in enormous cars and point.
Australia: Same as America.
Great Britain: Home at last! This is the best country in the World. London is the 4th largest city in the World. The Post Office Tower is 580 ft high, and Ben Nevis is 4,406 ft high. Gt. Britain is the 7th largest island in the Whole World! The Manchester Ship Canal is

the 6th longest inland waterway in the Whole World! And the 8th highest waterfall in the Whole World is named after King Edward VIII! Besides which the English Kings and Queens take up all of 4 pages in the Whitaker's Almanac, whereas French Presidents only take up ½ a page.

Lesson 3: Revision

Conclusion: Well, how did you get on with your Geography coarse? All you have to do now is pass the exam. To do this send £5 to Mr E. Stebbins
3, Hook Underpass
Ewell Surrey
You will receive a beautiful hand-decorated degree by return, plus full details of the 'E. Stebbins Global Religion' Plan (U.K.) Ltd.

DAMMIT!
DAMMIT!!!
DAMMIT.

film review
with Philip Jenkinson

HELLO THERE. One or two apologies to readers, first of all to the film buff who wrote in to correct me about something I said in my exhausting analysis of Von Sternberg and his impact on the cinema. Well I have checked, and yes you're quite right, you *can* still buy that wash-and-wear fabric for shirts at 'Guy's an' Dave's', Kings Road. Secondly there are so many films to look at this week that I'm afraid that the knitting pattern I promised you in the Michelangelo Antonioni profile will have to be held over until next time.

Above: 'I sit in the sun'. The Company
Below: 'I'll remind you to remind me. We said we wouldn't look back' Finale. Act 2. The Company

'SALAD DAYS' *Dir. Sam PECKINPAH 1972*

Drop what you've got on instantly and run across to your local, I can promise you you won't be disappointed. Sam Peckinpah has taken Julian Slade's light romantic musical comedy story of loveable young Oxbridge graduates making their way in the world, and added the magic ingredient: sadism. It's Peckinpah at his imaginative best; Minnie the magic piano becomes a symbol of Man's search for bloody violence, his natural desire to rip the skin off his neighbours and let their guts spill out on to the carpet in technicolour. 'We're looking for a piano' sing the boys chirpily in their sunlit Mathew Arnold world as they hack away at foaming limbs with the casual ease of a Smithfield butcher; 'Look at me I'm dancing' sings Jane ingenuously, adding a new irony to the line, as we see her entrails literally dancing out of her. It's a super movie. If you like violence – and who doesn't? – then this is for you.

Top 'I'm looking for a Piano'. Julian and the Company
Below: 'Anyone for Tennis?'. Simon, Veronica, Sandy and Paul
far Below: 'Still looking for a piano'. Graham

film news in brief

Michael Winner's latest film *The Con* is not a film to be missed. It's a film to be avoided at all cost.
Try if you can to visit Chabrol's *Butcher* at Ealing (his lamb chops are superb). There's an excellent documentary on The Making of *The Underwater Macbeth* (Dir: Jacques Cousteau. A Playboy Production)
and if you are in the mood you can still go and see Ken Russell's *Boyfriend* in the suburbs.

left: Michael Winner
Below: Underwater Macbeth'

'THE THIRD TEST MATCH' *Director Pier Paulo Pasolini 1972, Oval Films Ltd*

Just as Peckinpah has revealed the bloodthirsty violence bubbling beneath the skin of Edwardian man so, in a different way, Pasolini rips off the MCC tie to reveal the seething cauldron of sex that lies beneath the shirt. Once his Pandora's cricket box is opened we find flying out from the pavilions and changing rooms of the first-class counties a positive miasma of sexual yearning, culminating in the classic Brian Close shower scene, which recalls Hitchcock's use of Janet Leigh in a very similar shower (without, of course, the presence of Basil D'Oliveira).

Left: Umpire Syd Buller's controversial LBW decision at Edgbaston
above MCC v The Australians at Worcester

Above Enforcing the follow-on. Trent Bridge.
below England's batsmen in trouble on an Australian 'sticky'

'Sex and the Single Wicket Competition' could be the subtitle of this movie, for we get revealing glimpses of John Snow (a fine performance this on a desperately slow wicket) and we see quite a lot of the old Ken Barrington. Of course the bedroom scenes were bound to cause trouble, as they did during the making – Geoff Boycott walked out of filming a torrid 'innings' when he was on a pair at Headingley, and there were complaints from Alan Knott's Auntie – but on the whole, as Denis Compton has observed, the balance between bed and bat is well maintained.

Right: A rare picture of Pasolini at work, during filming of 'The Third Test Match'

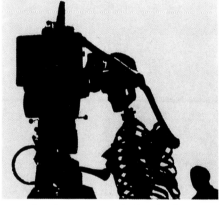

John Snow's devastating opening spell at Lord's against the Tourists. John Snow's amazing figures at Lord's

Pasolini shows us, surely for the first time, that M. J. K. Smith's finely-taken catch in the gulley to dismiss Newitt, was not merely the turning point of the entire Test Series, but a revelation of how successful worker co-operation can beat the power of advanced capitalism on the factory floor. In particular the portrayal of Cowdrey's inherently Marxist century at The Oval as the swansong of old-style Stalinism, set against Amis's rejuvenating Leninist duck, was a bold stroke from a seasoned director. For me cricket has never been so interesting.

'The Third Test Match' 1972 ('Di Combato Trinito Con Sexualis é nudo')
Pelham Warner Cinema, Leicester Sq.

Clive James Looks at the Cinema Screen

The movie that most moved me this month may make more money than multi-millionaire mystery-man hideaway Howard Hughes himself. It's a human interest picture: the sort that makes you concentrate on the usherette. Ouch. Joking apart, all motion picture addicts worthy of the name should pin back their eyeballs and take a celluloid shower in this one. If you can't tell the difference between Zsa Zsa Gabor, and you don't much care, it may not be exactly your cup of possum juice, but catch it if you can for the sheer magic of the Intermission which comes like a dose of clap in the middle of a mad month in a Melbourne cat-house. The name of the picture escapes me.

'Rayner's Lane' is a movie you'd be well advised to miss. And you'd be wrong. Go and see it. You'll be surprised. It's terrible. It's

definitely mutton dressed as Lady Caroline Lamb but I haven't had such an enjoyable time in the cinema since I spent four hours in a Sydney Drive-In and finally discovered it was a multi-storey car park. Ouch.

The same goes for 'The Con'. Don't miss it. Avoid it like the plague. But go anyway. You'll hate it. It's marvellous. It's Kafka in a sheep dip, an example of the Protestant Work Ethic on Rollerskates with enough acres of fresh flesh to bring a boyish smile to the frozen features of a case-hardened Bushman at an outback cattle auction. But enough – as Kierkegaard observed – is a treat. Don't take your family, take your mac. Personally I'd rather drink warm Fosters, but, as W. H. Auden said, 'It takes two to tango'. He should know. Ouch.

'Lovesick' makes 'Claire's Knee' look like a rare skin disease. Catch it at your peril. It's a skin-flic for dermatologists only. If you're an osteopath with a warped sense of humour and your own sauna bath, you might just like it. If not, be warned. Go and see it. You'll hate it. It's smashing. No sweat, but all armpit. Ouch. Like sodomy, it's fun once in a while but let's hope they don't make it compulsory. It's rather like being offered a choice between drowning to death in a cup of cold vomit, while eating skewered eyeballs, or being beaten about the brain with a de luxe edition of *Roget's Thesaurus* while nibbling at nourishing roast fingernails. Not a choice I'd care to make. But if pushed – plump for the fingernails. Goodnight. Ouch.

Rat Recipes

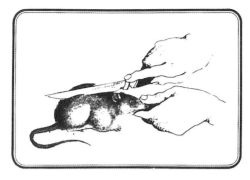

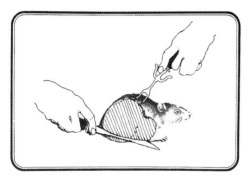

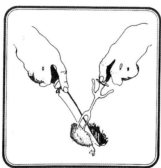

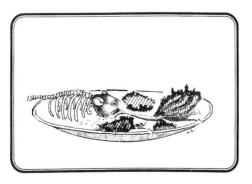

Rat pie:

Take four medium-sized rats and lay them on the chopping board. Having first made sure the chopper is freshly sharpened, raise it as high above the first rat as you can. Make sure that the rat's neck is well exposed, then bring the chopper down with as much force as possible onto the neck or head of the rat. Then cook it in a pie.

Rat soufflé:

Make sure that the rat's squeals are not audible from the street, particularly in areas where the Anti-Soufflé League and similar do-gooders are out to persecute the innocent pleasures of the table. Anyway, cut the rat down and lay it on the chopping-board. Raise the chopper high above your head, with the steel glinting in the setting sun, and then bring it down – wham! – with a vivid crunch – straight across the taut neck of the terrified rodent, and make it into a soufflé.

Bits of rat hidden under a chair:

This isn't so much a recipe as a bit of advice in the event of members of the Anti-Soufflé League or its simpering lackeys breaking into your flat. Your wife (or a friend's) should engage the pusillanimous toadies from the League in conversation, perhaps turning the chat to the price of corn and the terrible damage inflicted by all kinds of rodents on personal property, and rats attacking small babies (this always takes the steam out of them) and you should have time to get any rat-bits safely out of sight. Incidentally do make sure that your current copy of *The Rat Gourmet* hasn't been left lying around, otherwise all will be in vain, and the braying hounds of the culinary killjoys will be unleashed upon the things you cherish: your chopping-board, the chopper caught in the blood-red glare of the fading sun. Bring it down – crunch! The slight splintering of tiny spinal column under the keen metal! The last squeal and the death twitches of the helpless rat!

Chez Rat

Hors D'Oeuvres

Soup of the Day
(nearly always rat)

Melon Venezia
(succulent honeydew melon, soaked in Kirsch, with a dead rat on top)

Ratatouille

Escargot
(really rat)

Entrées

Rat au Vin
(fresh rat killed with a chopper held up against the glinting sunlight and brought down with a terrific wham! on the tiny vertebrae in wine)

Rat au Poivre
(the same only more violent)

Rat à Tué
(unlimited rats killed at your table by the method of your own choice)

Rat Muré
(large black rats hurled at a wall by the chef)

Dessert

Rats
(various)

Coffee and rats 40p extra

May we recommend to go with your meal some fine Australian wines which only real gourmets will appreciate.

1 **Black Stump Bordeaux**
A peppermint flavoured Burgundy.

2 **Sydney Syrup**
Can rank with any of the world's best sugary wines.

3 **Châteaublue**
Has won many prizes, not least for its taste, and its lingering afterburn.

4 **Old Smokey 1968**
Compares favourably with a Welsh claret.

5 **1970 Côtes du Rod Laver**
Recommended by the Australian Wino Society, this has a kick on it like a mule. Eight bottles of this and you're really finished. At the opening of the Sydney Harbour Bridge Club they were fishing them out of the main sewers every half an hour.

6 **Perth Pink**
The most famous of the sparkling wines. This is a bottle with a message in it and the message is 'Beware'. This is not a wine for drinking. It's a wine for laying down and avoiding.

7 **Melbourne Old and Yellow**
Another good fighting wine, which is particularly heavy and should be used only for hand-to-hand combat.

8 **Chateau Chunder**
An appellation contrôlée specially grown for those keen on regurgitation. A fine wine which really opens up th sluices at both ends.

9 **Hobart Runny**
For real emetic fans only. Should not be served during dinner.

10 **Prize-winning Chateau-bottled Cuve Réserve Nuits St Wogga-Wogga**
Has a bouquet like an abbrigine's armpit. A kind of contraceptive wine. A bottle of this will put sex right out of the question.

11 **Ainsley Gotto 1971**
'It wiggles, it's shapely and its name is Ainsley Gotto.' A fine wine this, that'll bring down any government.

12 **Australian Pommie Juice**
Eurghh. Export only.

13 **Beach Burgundy**
A surfing wine from the dunes. One glass of this and a Bondi lifeguard will give you the kiss of life all afternoon. Two glasses and even the sharks will have to look out. Warning to Sheilas: this one will certainly make you damp.

14 **Vieux Rolf Harris (Non-vintage)**
An older wine for the less discerning palate. A lot of sparkling confidence but no taste.

15 **A Bottle of Legeaupna**
A traditional Australian wine this that'll prize open the thighs of even the most reluctant Sheila. If the contents don't work you can always use the bottle.

Plus Two New Zealand Wines

16 **All Black Special. Brut Réserve**
From near Otago. Slightly worse than 'All Black Special' but all right for those difficult times when you haven't 'been for a while.

17 **1970 Chateau-bottled Mud**
Slightly brackish in taste but better than drinking mud.

Overland to the World

What's the point of going abroad if you're just another tourist carted around in buses surrounded by sweaty mindless oafs from Kettering and Coventry in their cloth caps and their cardigans with their transistor radios and their *Sunday Mirrors,* complaining about…

the tea – 'Oh they don't make it properly here, do they, not like at home' – and stopping at Majorcan bodegas selling fish and chips and Watney's Red Barrel and calamares and two veg and sitting in their cotton frocks squirting Timothy White's suncream all over their puffy raw swollen purulent flesh 'cos they 'overdid it on the first day'. And being herded into endless Hotel Miramars and Bellevueses and Continentales with their modern international luxury roomettes and draught Red Barrel and swimming pools

full of fat German businessmen pretending they're acrobats forming pyramids and frightening the children and barging in the queues and if you're not at your table spot on seven you miss the bowl of Campbell's Cream of Mushroom soup, the first item on the menu of International Cuisine, and every Thursday night the hotel has a bloody cabaret in the bar, featuring a tiny emaciated dago with nine-inch hips and some bloated fat tart with her hair Brylcreemed down and a big arse presenting Flamenco for Foreigners. And adenoidal typists from Birmingham with flabby white legs and diarrhoea trying to pick up hairy bandy-legged wop waiters called Manuel and once a week there's an excursion to the local Roman Remains to buy cherryade and melted ice cream and bleeding Watney's Red Barrel and one evening you visit the so called typical restaurant with local colour and atmosphere and you sit next to a party from Rhyl who keep singing 'Torremolinos, torremolinos' and complaining about the food – 'It's so greasy isn't it?' – and you get cornered by some drunken greengrocer from Luton with an Instamatic camera and Dr Scholl sandals and last Tuesday's *Daily Express* and he drones on and on about how Mr Smith should be running this country and how many languages Enoch Powell can speak and then he throws up over the Cuba Libres. And sending tinted postcards of places they don't realize they haven't even visited to 'All at number 22, weather wonderful, our room is marked with an "X". Food very greasy but we've found a charming little local place hidden away in the back streets where they serve Watney's Red Barrel and cheese and onion crisps and the accordionist plays "Maybe it's because I'm a Londoner".' And spending four days on the tarmac at Luton airport on a five-day package tour with nothing to eat but dried BEA-type sandwiches and you can't even get a drink of Watney's Red Barrel because you're still in England and the bloody bar closes every time you're thirsty and there's nowhere to sleep and the

kids are crying and vomiting and breaking the plastic ash-trays and they keep telling you it'll only be another hour although your plane is still in Iceland and has to take some Swedes to Yugoslavia before it can load you up at 3 a.m. in the bloody morning and you sit on the tarmac till six because of 'unforeseen difficulties', i.e. the permanent strike of Air Traffic Control in Paris – and nobody can go to the lavatory until you take off at 8, and

when you get to Malaga airport everybody's swallowing 'enterovioform' and queuing for the toilets and queuing for the armed customs officers, and queuing for the bloody bus that isn't there to take you to the hotel that hasn't yet been finished. And when you finally get to the half-built Algerian ruin called the Hotel del Sol by paying half your holiday money to a licensed bandit in a taxi you find there's no water in the pool, there's no water in the taps, there's no water in the bog and there's

only a bleeding lizard in the bidet. And half the rooms are double booked and you can't sleep anyway because of the permanent twenty-four-hour drilling of the foundations of the hotel next door – and you're plagued by appalling apprentice chemists from Ealing pretending to be hippies, and middle-class stockbrokers' wives busily buying identical holiday villas in suburban development plots just like Esher, in case the Labour Government gets in again, and fat American matrons with sloppy-buttocks and Hawaiian-patterned ski pants looking for any mulatto male who can keep it up long enough when they finally let it all flop out. And the Spanish Tourist Board promises you that the raging cholera epidemic is merely a case of mild Spanish tummy, like the previous outbreak of Spanish tummy in 1660 which killed half London and decimated Europe – and meanwhile the bloody Guardia are busy arresting sixteen-year-olds for kissing in the streets and shooting anyone under nineteen who doesn't like Franco. And then on the last day in the airport lounge everyone's comparing sunburns, drinking Nasty Spumante, buying cartons of duty free 'cigarillos' and using up their last pesetas on horrid dolls in Spanish National costume and awful straw donkeys and bullfight posters with your name on: 'Ordoney, El Cordobes and Brian Pules of Norwich' and 3-D pictures of the Pope and Kennedy and Franco, and everybody's talking about coming again next year and you swear you never will although there you are tumbling bleary-eyed out of a tourist-tight antique Iberian airplane after a

third attempt, and it sinks to its knees and haemorrhages all over the sand, they cut off its ears and give him them as a present while all the locals cheer and the tourists throw up and the intellectuals discuss Ernest Hemingway and Watney's Red Barrel, and Ken Tynan's latest glorification of the insanely bestial act you've just

Explanation of symbols

★★★★	A really topclass household. Entertaining, witty, spotlessly clean. Worth a detour
★★★	A good family. Several armchairs, no dogs. Worth a visit if you're in the area
★★★	An above-average household. Comfortable, hardworking, but poss Catholics or Nonconformists. Cheesey snack likely
★★	Ordinary family, but may have nasty dog. Pop in by all means. Cup of tea or weak coffee usual
★	Dull, mean, petty, abusive and drab. No refreshment. Lucky to get out alive

	Middle Class
Ⓒ	Communists
Ⓐ	Atheists
	Arsenal supporters

	Married, with husband
	Married, with husband away a lot
	Married, with husband on night-shift
	Not married, but with husband

AA	Non-drinkers
	Piss artists
	One or two members of family boring
	Entire family boring
	Grandmother living in
	Deaf grandmother living in
	No grandmother but dog living in
	Deaf dog living in
	Son in Rhodesian police
	Avoid curried snacks
	Avoid port we've had for ages
	Avoid Politics
	Keep legs crossed
	Don't mention photographs
	Dog
	Vicious dog
	Cat
	Vicious cat
£115 &	Guinea Pig
	Parrot
	Abusive parrot
	Deaf parrot
	Vicious abusive parrot, tending to side with dog
	Terrapin
	Vicious terrapin, but in kitchen

Swindon Wiltshire Map 24 19 Edworth Road *Swindon 262*	Mr & Mrs Grayson	41%

First reports of this middle-aged couple were not good, but since inclusion in the guide last year their standards have improved. Though Mr Grayson remains rather dull, his wife is well worth a visit if you're in the neighbourhood.

Swindon Wiltshire Map 24 21 Edworth Road *Swindon 701*	Mr & Mrs Rogers, Brianette & Granny	69%

A pleasant little family, Mr & Mrs Rogers are cheerful despite financial difficulties and always good for a chat. Brianette is a well-developed eighteen-year-old & Granny is deaf. Avoid the back sitting-room.

Worthing Sussex Map 18 88 Rockery Crescent *Worthing 204*	Mr & Mrs Potter	18%

An appalling couple, rude and short-tempered. Their kitchen is painted a frightful yellow and Mr Potter is an un-compromising Marxist.

Bletchley Bedfordshire Map 36 6B The Flats *Bletchley 9041*	Doreen & Arthur Henbison	80%

At last what Bletchley has lacked for years, a really exciting couple. Arthur is an ex-hypnotist, and Doreen in the WAAF. They introduced wife-swapping to the flats four years ago and now it's hard to get in. Must book – especially at weekends.

Continued

This Page is in Colour

Hello and Welcome to this wonderfully colourful page. Isn't it terrific! We're in colour, man. Wow! Doesn't that green just blow your mind? This is a great day in the history of printing. We've freed words from the chains of drab monochrome and liberated them into exciting colour. Just look at the thousands of things to do. You can make words look like what they're saying: rainbow, water, sunset, multi-coloured, sea side, patriotic. Zonk Zonk Fab. Zowee! You can alternate colours to make patterns in the sentences. What a boon for long passages of boring prose! No longer need they appear quite so dull. With colour they come alive on the page. Great, isn't it? You can also make the patterns themselves change colours. I'm really into that. It's too much. Freaky. green blue green blue green blue green blue green blue green blue You can anticipate the mood of the words. Zap! Zap! I'm feeling so blue / jealous / angry / sick Real names, too, take on a whole new meaning, whether they are real people: Graham Greene George Brown Mary Whitehouse historical figures: William of Orange, Erik the Red or fictional characters like: Scarlett O'Hara and David Copperfield. Heavy man!

And it's not just the alphabet, numerals too can let down their hair and go into vivid colour, along with all the other symbols: 2*!"/@ £6–&8'()?$^{13}_{44}$+ = %$\frac{1}{2}$.,:; lines of multicoloured hues ═══════════════════════ It's just amazing what you can do when once you put your mind to it and start liberating your thoughts from the restricting and narrow channels of monochrome. From now on things never need be the same. A whole new world is opening up before your eyes.

We apologise for the temporary loss of colour. We are working on the fault but will be continuing this page meanwhile in black and white.

Accountants can be liberated! Stockbrokers can present a myriad-hued portfolio for the benefit of investors, business letters can have terrific bounce put into them, oh yes, anything is possible once your eyes have been opened to the tremendous possibilities. Kerpow. Kerpow, Too much. Oh yeah. And now. A publishing first. We proudly present the world's first short story written specifically for colour!

Red Skies over the White Sea by S. J. Greenblatt

The sun rose suddenly over the blue water of the White Sea, disturbing the pale calm pallid world of dawn. The mud flats near the harbour and the long sandy beaches caught the early morning rays, and the fresh dew sparkled on the flowers and the fields of lush grass. The Chinaman felt suddenly sick as he looked through the stained glass window into the cool of the room. The wallpaper caught his eye first and then he noticed the blood on the floor. He followed the trail of blood as it led him past the swimming pool, through the morning glories and into the long grass, where he found the mangled remains of Dr Goldberg. The blood dripped off the corpse and spattered on to the grass, trickling away to form a little pool by the side of the pool. 'Ah so,' said the Chinaman.

'Not so fast Wong,' said the uniformed Policeman. 'You were always jealous of Goldberg. I'm taking you into custody.'

The sun glowed in the sky where Rita lay stretched out on the beach – naked. Beside her her blue polka dot bikini had just a trace of . . . blood.

THE END

Contents:

it was written by Michael Palin, Graham Chapman, John Cleese, Eric Idle, Terry Jones and also Terry Gilliam

was illustrated mostly by Terry Gilliam and a bit by Peter Brookes

was edited by Eric Idle

design and graphics by Kate Hepburn and also by Lucinda Cowell

was photographed by Roger Perry also Roger Last and Reinholdt Binder

more photographs from Camera Press, Hulton Picture Library, Barnaby Picture Library, the Mansell Collection and also Graphic House Inc

also one way and another associated: John Gledhill, Constance Booth, Ian McNaughton and Carol Cleveland

First published in 1973 as 'The Brand New Monty Python Bok' and in 1974 as 'The Brand New Monty Python Papperbok'

This edition published in 2007 by Methuen & Co Limited, 8 Artillery Row, London SW1P 1RZ

Printed in Hong Kong by New Era Printing

ISBN 13:   978 0 413 77642 6
ISBN 10:   0 413 77642 5

by Col. B. B. Wakenham-Palsh M.C., O.B.E.

Chapter 19

A Lucky Escape

The next day I decided to take my usual pre-breakfast 'stroll', as I used to call it, into the *majambi*, or jungle, to see if I could catch sight of the very rare 'Chukawati Bati' or Bird of Purgatory, which 'Trusty' as we all called our faithful native *ghabi* or guide had reported seeing the previous *latbani* (evening) while we were looking for Harry's leg.

I had only been 'strolling' along the *majambi* (jungle) *ortobam* (path) for a few minutes when I became aware of a large and rather fierce *fritbangowonkabwaki*, or lion, which was standing partially hidden in the *pteee*, or clearing. I had strayed so close to him, absorbed as I was in my ornithological *questi* (quest) that when the splendid old thing opened its massive *goti* (jaws) to roar, revealing as fine a *womba*, or set, of teeth as I have seen in an adult male, each one as *bewapsiptoof'tag* (sharp) as a Welshman's head, I could, without so much as leaning forward, have taken his magnificent uvula in my left hand. Taking advantage of my good luck, I did so, tweaked it hard, an old English colonial officer's *granwi*, or trick. The lion was rather bemused by my ploy, and so I was able to get in a couple of good straight lefts, keeping my guard well up, to his upper palate and follow them with a cracking good right cross, moving my weight into the punch (as old 'Buffy' Spalding had taught me so many years ago, prior to the needle match against Uppington when 'Spindly' Crabber got up off the floor six times so pluckily only just to fail to win the draw which would have halved the *batwel* or match), right into my opponent's mane. Then dancing back a couple of paces, I weaved about causing *fritbangowonkabwaki* to miss wildly with his crude haymakers while I notched up a few useful points with my left *swati*, or hand, and I soon found that by this simple strategy of keeping him from getting in close, where his mighty jaws could have done a lot of *nagasaki*, or damage, I could pick him off pretty much at leisure. In fact it was only after some *twenti* (20) minutes, by which time I was well in *rogambi* (front), that, after a particularly nifty sidestep, I happened to glance around the clearing only to discover that our contest was now being watched by a circle of some fifteen odd of *fritbangowonkabwaki's* chums, some of whom were already beginning to edge forward, manes bristling and teeth akimbo, towards our good selves.

It was the work of a moment to divine from their magnificent expressions that they were taking a decidedly partisan attitude to our match, and that they would have few qualms about joining in on my opponent's side if necessary; and so, judging that, if they did, they would eventually subdue me by sheer weight of numbers, I took the better part of valour, and feinting away from another of *fritbangowonkabwaki's* wild rushes, I got in a parting short jab to the base of his tail (not a blow I was proud of, although it put him down for several minutes, but which I felt was excused by the exigencies of the situation, due, after all, to the unsporting behaviour of his colleagues in the first place) before springing upwards towards a lowly hanging branch of an enormous *bwinda tree* (a species related distantly to our own *Elm* (elm), but easily distinguishable by its broad unevenly veined leaf, with its characteristic cheetah's paw shape, and the peculiar purple-ochre colour of the outer leaves of its *gimbi*, or buds), some fifteen feet above my head. I had leapt not a moment too soon, for, although I had gained a firm grasp upon the handy branch, two of *fritbangowonkabwaki's* pals, leaping with me, had each seized one of my trusty boots in their jaws whilst a third had succeeded in firmly embedding his *fangs* (teeth) in the seat of my pants, albeit not in my *sit-upon* itself, but in the surrounding material thereof. What a strange sight I must have made, hanging unshaven from the branch with three enormous lions attached to me! It was not, indeed, without difficulty that I pulled myself up until I could take the branch in my mouth, thus freeing my hands for the more important work of detaching the determined trio, whose bites, however, proved to be so *woki*, or vice-like, that I eventually decided, not without regret, that it was only by actually abandoning the relevant apparel that I could free myself of their attentions.

Unlacing a jungle boot while hanging by one's teeth from a tree with three angry lions attached is not as easy as it might seem, when the lions concerned are being urged on to even greater efforts by the highly vocal support of their companions beneath, but eventually it was done, and right boot and lion plummeted back into the clearing, followed rapidly by their opposite numbers. With the vastly reduced load the shorts were a formality and in a trice I was seated comfortably on the branch looking down at the enraged horde beneath, who by now, incidentally, must have numbered well over a hundred. I must say they were making a truly memorable *din* (shindy). However, I was feeling distinctly peckish by now, and so doffing my *sola topi* rather humorously in their direction I turned for home and breakfast, hoping *fritbangowonkabwaki* and company would lose interest in me if I stuck to the trees for the first couple of miles. Another old trick, or *granwi*.

Imagine my surprise, when I discovered sitting next to me on the branch, blocking my path, one of the largest *yumbotos* (Congolese gorillas) I have ever set eyes on, and I've seen a few in my time, including one old female at Chukambara, or New Bolton, who, in fit of *pique* (rage) brought on by being struck by lightning, tore an anvil in half much to everyone's surprise. It is said that his extraordinary strength, allied to his almost legendary short temper, makes *yumboto* the most feared creature in the whole of Africa, although many claim they will never attack a man unless he comes within three miles of them. Well, this fellow was certainly a magnificent specimen, with forearms as thick as a *poti's nangatwami*, or *sitpu*, and judging from the malevolent expression upon his face bad tempered to a fault. I handed him my *topi*, as a gesture of friendship, but he merely started poking holes in the crown of it with his index finger while looking at me in what seemed to be a deliberately significant way. With the lions below, this chap barring my way, and no other branch within leaping distance, I decided there was nothing for it but to sit tight and hope that something would turn up, but before I could put this plan into operation *yumboto* started edging towards me, and reaching for my head. I backed warily away towards the end of the branch, which served only to infuriate him further; the reason for which I soon discovered, when I bumped into a second gorilla, who had obviously been sitting between me and the end of the branch throughout, and who was equally obviously my pursuer's *mate* (wife). In a flash it became clear to me that he had interpreted my sudden arrival between them as an attempt to infringe their relationship, and my subsequent retreat from him as the first step in my campaign to win her favours. What an amusing notion! Time was running short, however, and so I formulated a ruse. If I could persuade the jealous husband to rush the last few inches towards me, it was possible that the branch would snap under our combined weight and activity and that I would then use the split second before we fell to employ him as a kind of vaulting horse, executing the simple half somersault 'Buffy' Spalding had taught me all those years ago, to gain the branch beyond him and above the point where it would probably break. I could then return to breakfast unhindered, as my erstwhile companions would be forced to continue their quarrel with *fritbangowonkabwaki* and his chums beneath. So I turned to *yumboto's* mate, slapped her bottom in a lewd sort of way, and planted a kiss full on her lips. This produced the required rush from *yumboto*, the branch snapped and everything went according to plan.

As I made my way back to camp through the trees some *jambotwanibokotwikatwanafryingpanibwanabotomafekazami* (five) minutes later I noticed to my surprise on the *majambi*, or *stakawi*, or *chittamba*, or jungle path below me not only the sixty or seventy lions who had been following me since I'd left the vicinity of the clearing, but also, hurrying along in the middle of this group, and peering constantly up at me, none other than *yumboto's* mate! From this I was able to glean that far from scrapping among themselves as I had hoped, *fritbangowonkabwaki's* pals and my gorillas had joined forces and were now pursuing me, as it were, hand in glove. At that moment I heard a sound behind me and, turning, I spotted, swinging through the trees towards me, *yumboto* and thirty or forty of the more agile lions. As luck would have it, I was at that moment within half a mile of the Wananga River and so I set off at full speed in its direction, reasoning that if I could find a convenient creeper straddling its surging waters I could reach the far bank, thus making further pursuit more difficult.

I had a head start and managed by brachiating, to hold my lead all the way to the river, where, to my delight, I spotted a solitary creeper suspended from a tree just upstream, across the cascading torrent, to the forest the other side. Ideal! Once I had crossed, I could destroy the only method of doing so, and complete my 'stroll' on foot. It was the work of a moment to gain the tree whence my creeper hung and soon I was well on my way towards the far bank, admiring the magnificent view of the raging Wananga directly beneath. Indeed I was not half-way across before I began to realise that my 'creeper' was not all it might be, and looking towards the far end of it I was astonished to see, staring back at me from a wak-wak tree, the unmistakable square head, yellow-green criss-cross markings and fearful fangs of an anaconda! I will admit I was astounded! An anaconda in Africa! How it could ever have found its way there from the banks of the Amazon, let alone why it should have been asleep in this strange position, I shall never know but—as I soon confirmed from the characteristic heptagonal scales and the suffused neutral colouring I was grasping—an anaconda it was, and one that clearly took exception to being demoted to viaduct. So with one mighty flick of its rippling body, I was sent spinning where I had to dodge a passing eagle, high, high up into the air, before being able to plunge downwards into the waiting *maelstrom* (river).

I had already surmised that my new surroundings would pose a different problem, for the Wananga is notorious both for the quantity of its hippopotamus and crocodile, and also for the degree of rancour with which these two species regard the human race, and sure enough, on surfacing, I saw the huge shapes of the former setting off towards me from their station upstream, while several thousand of the latter bore down on me from the other direction; so I struck out for the shore with a fast crawl and must have gone some fifty yards before I came up for my first breath, quite against old Algy Bartlett's sound advice to breathe regularly and look where you're going no matter what stage the race is at, which I forgot so disastrously in the three cornered match against Oundle and Haileybury when, after being almost ten yards up after eight lengths, I got so tangled up in the ropes separating the lanes that in the end I had to be content with fourth place and a solitary point. Anyway I paid for ignoring Algy's guidance because, when I surfaced only some ten feet from the shore, with the crocs and hippos hot on my heels, I found myself, to my disappointment, confronted by a line of gorillas and lions at the water's edge, *yumboto* and *fritbangowonkabwaki* well to the fore. In the excitement I had struck out for the wrong bank! What a pickle to put myself in! Still I had to make the best of a bad job, so I swam straight at the nearest crocodile, waited until he opened his enormous jaws and then quick as a flash spurted forward and, snatching a full lungful of air, hurled myself into his mouth, pulling the jaws shut after me, and scrambled down his throat, while he was still surprised, to the relative safety of his stomach, where I stayed, holding my breath, until I guessed the coast was clear. Then gambling all on a quick getaway, I worked my way back up his thorax and started insistently tickling the back of his throat. I did not have long to wait, for the jaws opened suddenly and I was hurled out into the light of day by the force of the mightiest cough I have ever experienced at such close quarters, right onto the bank of the river, believe it or not about 10 (ten) yards from the point where the rest of the fellows were just tucking into their devilled kidneys. I must say they were pretty amused to see me appearing from a nearby crocodile without my shorts, but I took their jesting in good part and had soon rejoined them to salvage what I could from the pan of kidneys.

It may seem that I have rather padded out a commonplace enough tale, but the real reason that I have recounted my adventure in perhaps rather unnecessary detail is that *exactly* the same thing happened to my wife the very next day.

How to....

**And how are you today?
Feeling really keen and excited?
Make sure your pencils are sharpened.
Put your spectacles on —
if you wear them that is. Right!
And off we go with today's lessons.**

No 1: **How to write fan letters**

Hello Fans! Now we'll try writing a fan letter – here are some examples for you:

Dear Barbra Streisand,
        Please could you send me your autograph and the name of your optician? I don't think you look odd at all. I enclose a stamped addressed envelope.
                        Yours sincerely,
                        . . . . (*insert name here*)

Dear Buckminster Fuller,
        I have followed your career with great interest, from the early days at Harvard and the Annapolis Naval Academy, your dark days as a Nat. Accounts salesman and your stint with the Kelly-Springfield Truck Co. in 1922, through the first excitement of your appointment as Assistant to the Director of Research and Development at the Phelps-Dodge Corpn., and the position of Chief Engineer at the Dymaxion Co. Inc., right up to your Presidency of Geodesics Inc. in '54. I have been greatly impressed by your energetic-synergetic geometry and your geodesic and tensegrity structures, particularly the 2000 domes for the U.S. Marine Corps and U.S. Navy. Of your books, *Ideas and Integrities* (1963) and *Education Automation* (1963) have influenced me a great deal and helped me form my current appraisal of environmental and architectural problems. So please! please! Could you send me a signed photo and one for my sister who also thinks you're fab!
                        Yours dreamily,
                        . . . . (*insert name here*)
P.S. Did you *always* used to wear spectacles?

Dear Lord Thomson of Fleet,
        I think you and your newspaper empire are really great.
                        Yours,
                        . . . . (*insert name here*)
P.S. Can you really SEE through those spectacles?

Dear Maxwell Joseph,
        I really think you are dishy and your policy of acquiring an enormously large number of companies under your own personal control makes me go all gooey.
                        Yours dreamily,
                        . . . . (*insert name here*)
P.S. They *are* contact lenses, aren't they?

No 2: **How to become a Segas employee**

This isn't as difficult as it sounds. Every year, thousands of people become Segas Employees without restraining their limbs or even changing their religious convictions for a set of outworn socio-political theories. So – how to do it?

Well, the Chairman of Segas is Mr R. N. Bruce O.B.E., and he's ever such a nice man. Write to him and tell him how much you'd like to become a Segas employee. Of course, you must remember that he earns between £9,900 and £11,200 per year, so don't go inviting him round to dinner or anything like that . . . a cup of tea in the Segas Employees' canteen would be safer than exposing your home to his ridicule. One final tip: whatever you do, *don't* write to Sir Henry Jones (he's Chairman of the Gas Council) because he earns £20,000 a year *and* gets £1,000 a year expenses – so just think of the social gaffes you could make with him!

Well, there you are! If you're really serious about becoming a Segas Employee, nothing will stand in your way. If your first attempts do not succeed, then you'll try again and again. Remember, every Segas Employee had to start somewhere, and not all of them had the advantage of reading this!

No 3: **How to have lunch with the Queen**

This isn't so easy. I won't make any bones about it – I haven't succeeded and I doubt if you will. In fact there isn't much advice one can give – you can try writing to the Queen's Private Secretary (Lt.-Col. Rt. Hon. Sir Michael Adeane) but you'll probably only get a short note saying She's otherwise engaged, and it probably won't even be signed by Sir Michael, only one of his clerks like Miss Coulton or Miss Reid.

The fact is, it's very difficult to get to talk with the Queen at all. It's not that she doesn't like talking – I mean every time you see her she's talking to someone – but to be quite honest with you, I think she's just a tiny-weeny bit choosey about *who* she talks to . . . not that she hasn't every right to pick her own friends in her own way, but one can't help feeling she's missing out on a lot of interesting conversations by being so snooty about having lunch, especially when I'd made arrangements for us to get into the Segas Employees' Canteen on a day when they had chicken risotto on the menu. *

* For further information on chatting up Queens etc. see Python Book Of Etiquette.

No 2 Again: **How to rub your stomach up against a famous T.V. Personality**

This is another difficult one, unless you can get into a crowded situation with one (e.g. a tube or bus during the rush hour).

The thing is to choose your famous T.V. personality (say: Richard Baker or Cliff Michelmore) then bare your stomach – if it's cold put a mac over it, or hold some newspapers in front of it, then discover where the Famous T.V. Personality of your choice is working. You go along there, and wait until you see the Famous T.V. Personality of your choice go into a gents, then follow them in holding the newspaper in front of your bare stomach and . . . (*The remainder of this section has been withdrawn on legal advice.*)

No 5: **How to rub your stomach up against a traffic warden**

This is much easier. I've done it myself on numerous occasions. Hold the newspapers in front of your stomach, until the traffic warden approaches the meter where you're crouching. Then, as he draws level with you, fling the papers aside and spring up with a mighty yell and rub your stomach up against him. Surprise is the essence of this method, and I personally don't recommend it if you have bladder trouble.

No 6: **How to rub your stomach up against a chair leg**

This one's terribly easy. Oh it's so simple it's really a dead cinch! I've done it just now – there! Just after I wrote that I did it again. It's potty! Anyone could do it . . . the only point to watch for is that Mrs Stebbins doesn't come in while you're doing it, because she's a bit apt to criticize and it's not easy to find another place at £2.50 a week just because your landlady had a misguided upbringing and never learnt about certain things until she met Mr Stebbins and that was a bit of a shock. Anyway, must stop now, as the gas has just run out. My next series of articles will include:

How To Find 5p In The Dark
How To Nurse A Toe
How To Become Marlon Brando's Speech Therapist (*another difficult one*)
How To Knock Over Sir Alec Douglas-Home (*difficult*)
How To Burn A Piece Of Paper (*easy*)
How To Measure Tony Jacklin's Inside Leg (*very difficult indeed*)

No 7: **How to read**

Reading is easy. If you can read this you will know how easy it is. There are just 4 simple things to remember and you will be able to read:

1) **Don't** drop the book.
2) **Don't** start reading before you open the book.
3) **Don't** shut your eyes when reading.
4) **Don't** cover the book with a rug or blanket while reading it.
5) There is **no** point five.

Once you've mastered the art of reading, like I did, a whole new world will open up before you. You will begin by being able to decipher basic word combinations – *Daily Express* editorials, cheese labels and shoe box sizes. Then comes the world of the Public Library, where I work. Wow! Ye-hey! Woweee! Oweeeeee!

... miserable pittance they got for the privilege of having a thirty-floor hotel built in their front garden: and he tries to tell you about God, and Churchill and comradeship in the army and he puts his hand on your thigh and starts crying and talking of loneliness and passes out while the tourists titter and the Scotsman at the bar offers you a choice between his drinks bill or your hospital bill and you finally stagger out and get picked up by some English cow who hasn't had it for months, who smells like a distillery and who's leaping out of her clothes in all directions, and she tugs at your belt muttering about holiday romance and all the Spanish brandy she's had so that she's got an alibi in the morning, and then coaxes your brewer's droop into vague interest long enough for her to leap all over you shivering and moaning and biting your ears and squealing "Otto! Otto!" the name of the coach driver on her last package holiday who got so drunk he went up to her room and then had to climb out the window when he saw what the goods were like. . . .

HI THERE, TIGER!

Useful Advice

I've had letter after letter after letter after one particular letter which asked, 'What should I do about my appendix on the Piccadilly Line?' — Well Miss N., I can only assume you're talking about an acutely inflamed vermiform appendix. The answer simply is — take it out. I've no wish to give glib advice — I know there are bound to be difficulties for the inexperienced layman or woman, contemplating auto-appendicectomy. One tiny hint here — have a good rummage through your handbag and make sure your Lane's forceps are not caked up with biscuit crumbs, bits of fluff, old bus tickets etc., it could save an awful lot of fuss later on. I have set out a few details you will find opposite which may help you, and a Lines and Stations Index which will be useful Remember that stations marked † are open on weekday rush-hours only, stations marked * are closed Saturdays and Sundays.

Having found any open Underground station, study your diagram and find the blue line marked 'Piccadilly' in the key. Select a station appropriate to the severity of the inflammation e.g. mild or grumbling appendicitis you could start at Hammersmith, being careful NOT to change at Earl's Court and comfortably have incised your abdomen and exposed the inflamed organ by the time you are between Knightsbridge and Hyde Park Corner, having up to Leicester Square left to complete your excision. The six minutes between there and King's Cross gives you plenty of time to be completely sewn up before the terminal at Cockfosters — a very unpleasant place to be with a gaping abdominal wound (and a plastic bucket full of evil smelling viscera).

Points to Remember

1. If you are at all uncertain please ask the ticket inspectors about gridiron incisions. They are fully trained public servants and are most helpful.
2. The Piccadilly Line stops running at 11.50 am.
3. For severe inflammation consult the London Transport Information Centre and choose one of their longer journeys – arranging it so that the actual excision of the inflamed viscus takes place somewhere along the length of (say) the Bakerloo Line (20·84 miles). Or you might try a shuttle up and down the Victoria Line (light blue) for pre- and post-operative treatment, convalescing on the Circle Line (yellow).
4. Red Rovers may not be used on the Underground – nor can they be bought on buses, or in hospitals.

Finally a few words of warning:

Whatever you do remain calm at all times. Do not throw used swabs on to the floor of the carriage – these can cause delay or prevent successful operation of the automatic doors. A purse-string suture should be inserted into caput caeci about half an inch from the base – and failure to surrender a valid ticket at the end of your journey could mean a fine of up to £100 for a first offence.

Join the Dots

DIRECTORY

Roy Jenkins
'Europe's favourite'.
Tip Top Talent Agency.
Blackpool.

Norman Mailer
3 Acts. 6 gorgeous girls.
Own car. Own bottle. Still some years free.
c/o Oxfod Artistes

Clive Jenkins
'The Welsh Prince of Laughter'.
With hilarious audience participation
Exclusive Management, ASTMS Enterprises.

Richard Baker
'Lemon Curry?'
Comedy Imps. Cabaret. Newsreading.
Sole Agents: Kendall & Dougall.

Footplatemen
Available for private Clubs.
Spec Acts. etc.
T.U.C. Acts Ltd.

Karl Mildenburger
Now in Cabaret
at Lyme Regis. 'Talk of
Lyme Regis', Charmouth,
Nr. Lyme Regis.

Humphrey Burton
'The' Comedian for the mixed Occasion.
Funny voices. Dog act alive.
'Fills the stage with flags.'

A. J. Ayer
'A song, a smile, and a logical inconsistency.'
'Super'. The Philosopher.
Still some weekends free in August.
c/o Oxfod Artistes.

Anthony' Barber and Jane Russell
'A song, a Chancellor and a good time'
Both still alive.

'Trevor' Roper and his incandescent Poodle
Lectures on the English Civil
War with Amazing Dog Tricks.
Contact: Oxfod Artistes.
STILL AVAILABLE FOR
PANTO: L. Rowse and Betty
Warden Sparrow - Mediaeval
Bird Impressions

Frank Sinatra
wishes to be known as
ARTHUR BRIGGS

Norman Boils FAT & FUNNY
wishes to be known as
Norma Boils

Ian Smith
is now invading Poland
Crowd work available

AMAZING VENT ACT!
Sam Peckinpah and 'Roger'
'It still talks
with the
head sawn off'
'brilliant' Sunday Times
'terrible' Sunday Times
'banal' Stan Mortensen
AND GALA ATTRACTIONS

Indira Ghandi
(no relation)
Indian Political Impressions
'I laughed and laughed' R. Kray (no relation)
'Banal'. Stan Mortensen, Stuart Surridge,
Alec and Eric Bedser (no relations)

TRICKY DICKIE
'Thanks a million fellers'
Another four great years.
Bookings: White House Artistes.
Cables W.H.A.T

The Royal Arab Ballet
has vacancies for pilots and qualified
technicians.

Metropolitan Police
First class dog act.
'Dull isn't it?'
Available singly or in groups. Substances
extra. METPOL ARTISTES. WH1 1212.

Ian Smith (no relation)
Eats budgerigars. No feathers, no claws.
Amazingly vicious act.

Jonn 'Parrot-Face' Davies 'Europe's Own'.
'Future dates: 'Oasis', Rochdale.
'Talk of Sutton Coldfield',
'Caesar's Palace', Huddersfield.
'Top Ten Ballroom', Cairo.

THE UNDISPUTABLE
HUW WHELDON
Well and truly all your own.
'The voice and legs of a star.'

Georges Pompidou
Leicester's own.
'Your favourite frog' Wee Georgie Wood,
The Stage.
c/o FROG ARTISTES, PARIS.

Alan Whicker
An angel's voice and the Devil's wit.
Own Yacht.
ALAN WHICKER ARTISTES.

S. J. Gumby
wishes it to be
known that in
future he will be
known as
S. J. GUMBY.

THE SENSATIONAL
Mr Peter Walker
Mentalist & Sauna
Bath Act. 'Redevelops
before your very eyes'
SLATER-ARTISTES

Mr Julian Amery
formerly Mr Geoffrey Rippon.
c/o HEATHMEN ARTISTES.

M. Drabble
Now in Panto, West Hartlepool.

E. Heath
Weekly Rep. a Speciality.
Novelty Number.
Own evening dress.
Available for Parties.

David Frost
Still alive.
SLATER-PARADINE PRODUCTIONS LTD.

Teddy Johnson and Pearl Carr
Now available for Parliament.
Sole Agent: The Liberal Party.

'Emanuel Shinwell'
would like to thank the Grade Organisation
for a successful parliamentary career.

'Hello Folks'
F. R. Leavis
Arts Theatre,
Cambridge.

Russel Harty
Exotic dancer.
c/o SIMON DEE ARTISTES, LWT.

The Department of the Environment
wishes to change its name to
The Ministry of Trade and Industry
Still some weekends free in government.
Contact: Slater-Heath Ltd.

'Can ye hear me missus?'
Graham Greene
The Comedians. Granada TV.

Norman St. John Stevas
For all the family.
'Gaytime'. Harlow.

CHANGE OF MANAGEMENT
Terence Rattigan
is now with Chelsea Football Club.

Australia's Own
Clive James
Impersonations. Book Reviews. Beard biz.
AUSSIE ARTISTES, or via Rolf Harris.

Robin Day
Live at 'The Departure Lounge', Heath Row.
'Robin had to do that very awkward spot just
before Bingo. However he went quite well.'
Club Call, The Stage.

Hughie Green
Vacant Sundays.
Book for stag, clubs, parties etc.
Own Teeth.

ANNOUNCEMENT
Joan Bakewell
wishes to make it clear that
she is not related in any way
to William Whitelaw.

HRH The Pantomime Princess Margaret
Now available for openings, tours etc.
Own husband.

Marcel Proust
Internationally famous artiste.
Accompanies himself
on the Hammond
Organ.
Summer Season
Algeria.

Arthur Penis
wishes to change his name.
Will all his friends please note
that in future he will be known professionally
as ART PENIS.

The London Demolition Company
wishes to thank the Department of the
Environment for all the work.
Next bookings: Covent Garden, Piccadilly,
etc.

Clifford Irving
Out Soon.

'Another Great Year'
The Mafia
Sole Agents:
Luigi Vercotti.

Peter Dimmock
'Still going strong.'
BBC CLUB, Doncaster.

Boris Spassky Ltd.
Vent. Act. Yodelling etc.
Exclusive Management.

THE BBC
would like to thank the Governmer.t
for a successful engagement, and look
forward to a new season.

Katie Boyle
Merci, prego
und
dankershoen

THE MCWHIRTER BROTHERS
'A smile, a song, and a
lawsuit.' Now available
Contact: for publicity.
Guinness Artistes.

Richard Attenborough
(Hopefully 'Sir' soon.)
Not available 1973/4

DIS O'CONNOR
The English
Mox Bygraves.
Comodian,
songer and
dunceman.

Hugh Heffner
and 'Victor' Now in Panto at Avignon.
High Class act. Plus girls. 'Jest for kicks'.

The Pirhana Brothers
Doug & Dinsdale.
Fully booked until 1985*
*subject to parole.

SAMMY DAVIS JNR.
wishes to thank
R. M. Nixon Inc,
for the work.
NIXON ARTISTES,
WHITE HOUSE
CORPS.

The Pope
'Oo you are kind' Panto, Huddersfield.
Exclusive Management. Vatican City.
Telegrams: MAFICAN, ROME.

STILL
UNEXPECTEDLY
AVAILABLE
'Reggie'
R.E.F.A. Artistes Ltd. or
Poulson Agencies.

Ramsay MacDonald Change of Name (late Harold Wilson)
wishes to inform his old
friends of his new name

NOTE:
You Should Contact Equity if
you are approached by any of
the following:
A big chap in an expensive suit
offering free holidays in Rio.
Lord Hailsham (late Quintin Hogg.
Even later Lord Hailsham)
Holiday Near Ice (not Holiday on
Ice)
Holiday Upon Ice Ltd. (not Holiday
Through Ice Ltd.)
Holiday under Ice. (not Holiday in
Glamorgan Ltd.)
Ron Brothel Artistes
Ivan Crook (also Ivan Robber, Ivan
Thief, Ivan Stealer, Ivan Cheat and
Ivan Neverpay)
The Syd Cutler Vibro-Massage and
Assisted Shower Acting Troupe
Hailsham on Ice
(not Lord Holiday)   Cont'd....

Nude Auditions: Note
At all auditions for which 'you are
required to be naked, a bona fide Equity
representative must be present to have a
peek too.

Simulated Sex Acts: Note
You are not required to simulate the sex
act at auditions. However you may
undertake to simulate the sex act after the
audition at the home of a bona fide
producer providing he subsequently offers
you employment.

Stimulated Sex Acts:
You may not be required to simulate
orgasm at auditions. However if you have
a genuine one then you must inform
Equity in writing.

EXTRA WORK IN NUDE SCENES
You are not to do any
''extra'' work in nude scenes.
If you fail to give a
'performance' then this will
be termed a walk-on, and
you should ask the Stage
Manager to give you a chitty.

9

Its Probably Not Worth Joining

The Albert Hall during this year's Annual General Meeting

Are you less than interested in joining a society which has been a modern success story of unremitting lethargy, rapidly growing indifference and superbly increasing stagnation?

In this day and age there's very little an apathete can't do if he really hasn't made up his mind if he wants to or not.

So, why not fail to enrol today?

Write for details to our Secretary (or is it the Treasurer?) at:

The Headquarters of the British Apathy League,

Somewhere in Connaught Square, London. (Or is it Edinburgh?)

Our Chairman Writes:

Hello Apathetes everywhere. It gave me so much pleasure to see such a bad turn-out at this year's Annual General Meeting at the Albert Hall, and I want to thank everyone who was unable to attend. I'm afraid that, owing to illness, I was present at the occasion, but even so it was gratifying to see how many of you weren't able to make it.

Thanks again and let's see if we can't get an even lower turn-out at next year's meeting, details of which we are probably not going to send out soon. I for one will definitely be absent in July from the Annual Dinner Dance (tickets 25 gns). Response to this has been encouragingly sluggish and Mrs Carter tells me we haven't yet sold *one* ticket. I don't want to be too optimistic as the Box Office is still open, but I am hoping we can beat last year's effort, when only the Guest Speaker arrived. This year, incidentally, we've invited Frank Muir, and he's promised that commitments permitting he'll not be there on the 18th.

One small word of reproach; somebody has sent in a motion for next year's AGM proposing 'That there shall be no motions at next year's AGM', which does, I'm afraid, contravene Rule 23 of the League, 'That there shall be no motions at the AGM'. Now, as Chairman, I am prepared to overlook this, if the person responsible fails to get in touch with me by May (or June).

One final note of good cheer, there has been such a wonderfully lukewarm response to the special offer of Badges, Ties and Scarves, that the shop has had to send them back.

I would like to thank you all for your continuing uninterest in the business of the Society, without your whole-hearted inertia the League would not be where it is today, and I wish you every success in your private vegetation and public apathy.

Yours slothfully,
Miles G. erm

Mr Frank Muir who has again agreed to be absent this year.

I am not interested in joining **The British Apathy League.** Please do not enrol me or send me any information about the Society.

Cut this out and do not bother to post it. It's the thought that counts.

LET'S TALK ABOUT BOTTOMS

Hello! Some people don't like talking about bottoms, but I'm one who does. I think bottoms are super! Mine's a little beauty – I can feel it now as I sit on it. Wow! What a shame you can't see it, but I'm not showing it to *anybody* at the moment, because it's got a little spotty bit round the corner, and I don't want people saying I can't look after my own so what right have I got to talk about anyone else's. But take my word for it – it's like a little Michaelangelo *soaked* in Brut. Anyway the point is why's everybody so quiet about their bottoms? I mean there's Vic Feather, probably sitting on a peach but does he give anyone else a peek? Not on your life. And that Hugh Scanlon – he's just the same – never even mentions bottoms from one industrial dispute to another. I don't know about Jack Jones's of the T.G.W.U., I'd like to be more confident in myself before I had a peek at his, though I'm sure it's really lovely.

Jeremy Thorpe's bottom hasn't had much exposure either recently and I'm *sure* it's nice – you know, *really* nice – the kind that could easily spark off a Liberal revival. And the same with Margaret Thatcher – I'm *positive* that if *only* she'd show her bottom a few times, she'd do *such* a lot of good, and help people forget about their shabby lives. Anyway, Margaret, love, don't let them talk you out of it – if you *want* to show your bottom to a wider public, you go ahead, and show the moaning minnies on the back bench what a bit of bottom can do.

Well, it's time to close again. I've got to lift my bottom off the chair and take it round to the Valderma. So long, loves, let it breathe!

Hobbies

PEN PALS WANTED

Amalgamated Society of Locomotive Engineers and Firemen require pen pals either sex, in the Transport and General Workers' Union.

Pen Pals Wanted for Footplatemen, A.S.L.E.F. Executives, and Shop Stewards in the Coventry area. Write Mr Larch. Box 348, Hastings.

United Stokers, Boilermakers and Allied Trade Operatives require pen pals in the Bristol region. Interests: Camus; the development of the concept of 'thisness' from Duns Scotus to Gerard Manley Hopkins; oral sex.

Medical Officer of Health in the Gloucester area seeks genuine friendship with footplateman. Box 209.

Signalmen, Guards and Allied Trades require pen pals. No footplatemen.

PEN PALS, PROGRAMMES ETC.

Football programmes wanted urgently, especially Millwall, East Fife and Raith Rovers, by Head of Religious Broadcasting BBC Norwich. Will swap for old and current issues of The Churchman, The Christian Science Monitor, The Catholic Voice and Arsenal programmes.

Pen Pal will swap programmes with anyone keen on footplatemen. Box 238.

Stamps, Stamps, Stamps

Lonely philatelist seeks similar to share stamp hinges, Stanley Gibbons Catalogues, and bed-sit in Ipswich. Keen on French Cols, Lichtenstein, San Marino and Bondage.

STAMPS, PROGRAMMES, PEN PALS

Gentle footplateman, seeks genuine kind and considerate bachelor in the Transport and General Workers' Union for correspondence, and 'swaps' of stamps, football programmes etc. Only genuine applicants need apply. And that means not you Kevin. You needn't bother to come near me again. Please do not try and contact me in any way ever. Box 2093. After 6.

Miscellaneous

● The Choir. Organist Mr G. Rutter. Urgently needed for the choir; altos, trebles, tenors and footplatemen.

● *Hornby Dublo News.* The next meeting of the Parliamentary Hornby Dublo Society will be cancelled unless the person responsible returns the missing rolling stock and points to the Hornby Dublo Room (next to the Committee Rooms) immediately. R. Maudling, Hon. Sec.

The Model Boat Club Outing to the Official Barbican Strike has been postponed for a fortnight. H. Beach, Tres.

Have you a spare room for an Archbishop? Any Kenyan Asian interested in helping please contact Barry Ryan.

FOOTPLATEMEN, BOILERMAKERS, WATER TUBE AND ALLIED TRADES DEBATING SOCIETY

T.U.C. Debate, Thurs. Transport House. Motion 'That this house would legalise pot forthwith' proposed by Ass. Sec. of Amalgamated Miners' Union, seconded by Gen-Sec. of A.E.U., opposed by N.U.R. spokesman, and Father of the Whitehall Chapel of N.A.T.S.O.P.A.

STAMPS OR PROGRAMMES EXCHANGED

Footplatemen will exchange junior footplateman for stamps or programmes. South Shields Branch.

'Bulky' of Leicester. I've lost your address. Please write to 'Pliant Jim' of Doncaster, via Amalgamated Engineering Union, Sunderland.

Rip offs, Sell Out, Footplatemen etc.

Hand-made leather garments. Would suit young footplatemen. Ring Jennifer, Leeds.

Crashpads for Boilermakers and Allied Trades urgently needed in the Torquay area.

Footplateman busted at Durham Miners Gala, needs eyewitnesses to arrest quickly. Contact Keith. Leicester.

G. Nabarro would like pen-pal, preferably footplateman, in the Worcester area.

PAGE 71

Page 71 disappoints

'They failed to set the Thames on fire' might be the epitaph for this page – writes our Page 71 Correspondent. Disappointment greeted last night's unveiling of this the latest in a series of humorous pages, for alas Page 71 fails to live up to the promise of some of its predecessors. One immediately thinks of Page 58, or the splendid production of Page 19, or even the glories of the early 30's. It's not the last of the pages by a long chalk, but it certainly indicates signs of weakening, a post-coital feeling hovers over the writing, we have been here before and in rather better days.

Well I liked it

CLAIMS NON-NAZI.

INTERVIEWED at his Surrey hideaway a Mr Mart Tinbor-Mann said that he very much enjoyed the controversial Page 71. 'It's about time minorities were catered for, or done away with' he said.

After Page 71 the offices of Eyre Methuen were flooded with telephone call. The Chairman said later that it was a wrong number.

Protest over ~~re~~ ~~~~tion

Clive James on Page 71

Pardon my multiform metaphorical mishmash but I've just had my brain cells wiped and my mind's as out of place as a boiled egg in a Koala bear's bum. You might be well advised to miss Page 71. And wrongly. Don't read it. You'll love it. It's awful. But enjoyable. You'll be appalled. It's terrific. Wow. As W. H. Auden said, 'Good evening mother.' Indeed. Personally I found its combination of ~~~~ooky and kitsch, with just a touch of ~~K~~ierkegaard under the armpits, as incongruous as Marcel Proust muff-diving on the ~~~~dney sands, or Dame Nelly Melba as an ~~~~cream in an Esther ~~~~

OH WHAT A LET-DOWN !

Page 71
The Brand New Monty Python Bok

Oh, oh, oh, what a disappointment! After all the hullabaloo Page 71 turns out to be about as tough and biting as a weekend tea-party in a hostel for retired eunuchs. This is a genuine flag-flapping flopperoo. Such a public suicide hasn't been seen since that elderly lady flung herself under the King's horse to let the second favourite win the Derby.

BUS REBELS TO WORK ON

STOP PRESS

BBC Film Sensation

The BBC's massive budget prestige co-production with *Time-Life* of Page 71 of *The Brand New Monty Python Bok*, starring Helmut Berger, Tim Brooke-Taylor, Sophia Loren, Omar Sharif, and the Young Generation, scheduled for filming in Africa, South America, Southern India and parts of Burma, for eight months from April at a cost of £100,000, has been cancelled a Light Entertainment spokesman said today.

Quite amusing, not enough so.

Robin Barlar at the opening of Page 71:

One had heard so much of this page that perhaps one was looking for something a little more original. There was just a touch of familiarity about the jest, a kind of 'recherche à la temps perdu', or rather a more sadly stated 'mais où sont les neiges d'antan' cri de coeur, a squeal of Angst from a soul full of Mittelschmerz.

OH WHAT A LOVELY BORE

At last night's Page 71: SO MUCH for satire, boys. Personally I'd rather eat a can of stewed prunes and be banned from the lavatory for life again. They finally let the cat out of the bag and it turned out to be a dead duck. It's a no-no. A no-go, no-way lulu. A genuine egg-laying boo-boo, and when this egg hits the fans it's my guess they'll burn this book in their hundreds.

April 19, 1973

Property Developers to ~~~~ ~~~~ ~~~~over Page 71?

IRATE property developers are hopping mad with what they consider an all-out attack on their integrity by Eyre Methuen's latest Page 71. A Mr Jim Bulldozer of Slater-Bulldozer said that they were not taking legal action, but they were considering demolishing Eyre Methuen to make way for a high rise Office Block. When informed that Eyre Methuen was a high-rise Office Block a Mr Jim Gumby of Slater-Gumby started to moan quietly and sing in Welsh. A man is helping police with their decorating.

They were standing under a cloud, each with an arm round the other's neck, and Alice knew which was which in a moment because one of them had "DILL" embroidered on the collar and the other "DO".

"It's rude to stare" said the one marked Dill.

"And don't play with yourself" added the one else marked Do.

"Why ever not?" said Alice. "If you've no one else to play with..."

"Makes you blind" said Tweedledum.

"Stunts your growth" said Tweedledo "and makes you mad."

"What a strange land" thought Alice, gently pushing open the door of the White House.

"Have you been invited to the Orgy?" shouted Tweedledill.

"I'm sure I have" said Alice, and found herself inside a large Soup Kitchen, entirely filled with bowls of soup, and in one corner a Pig Policeman sat rocking a small bidet in his arms.

"Hush" said the Pig Policeman. "You'll wake the bidet" and he began to sing in a very loud voice.

The Walrus and the Carpenter,
Were walking hand in hand.
If only, said the Carpenter,
The Law would understand.

"Could you tell me the way to the Orgy?" Alice enquired politely when he paused for breath, but the Pig Policeman was singing so loudly and banging the tiny bidet with his truncheon so violently that at last Alice got up and pushed open a door marked "Window".

"Curious" said Alice, looking around a room lined full with Books and Magazines. Beside her was a Bookshelf labelled "Curious" and beside that a shelf labelled "Curiouser and Curiouser", and further down, right at the end of the room was a little door with a sign on it saying "Something stronger". But what attracted her attention most of all was a Pack of Interesting Playing Cards busily scampering around with scissors hacking desperately away at each other.

92

"What on earth are you doing?" enquired Alice, in a loud voice, for they were very preoccupied.

"We're trying to cut out the dirty bits of course," said the Two of Clubs.

"We always used soap and water for that" said Alice, "at least in the Nursery."

"Soap and water won't get rid of filth like this," said the Knave of Hearts, desperately lunging at himself with the scissors.

"But you'll do yourself an injury," said Alice, grabbing at the Ace of Spades just in time to prevent him cutting off a large piece.

"That's nothing to what'll happen if the Drag Queen finds us. Just look at this," and at that the Knave of Hearts showed her his body.

They must be really quite frightened, thought Alice, to cut away the pictures of those ladies and gentlemen. Just then she felt a nudge in the small of her back, and a little voice whispered in her ear, "Eat me," and she spun around so suddenly that she scattered the Pack of Interesting Playing Cards all over the place.

"Now look what you've done," complained the Nine of Diamonds, but before they could pick themselves up there was a great blaring of trumpets and in a whirl the Drag Queen herself arrived.

"What on earth's that?" screamed the Drag Queen in a dread voice, as the unlucky Playing Card trembled before her.

"Please, your Majesty..." stuttered the Knave of Hearts reddening.

"It most certainly does not please my Majesty" thundered the Drag Queen in a terrible voice. "Off with his nuts!" And at this the unfortunate Knave was dragged away while all the courtiers sang

Oh the Knave of Hearts
He had some tarts
All on a summer's day
And four and twenty black birds
Or at least that's what they say...

"Silence!" roared the Drag Queen.

"Please eat me" said a little voice in Alice's ear.

93

Did you know....
that El Greco's real name was E.L.Grecott?
Chuck Berry wrote many of Shakespeare's plays?
the Everly Brothers turned down a knighthood?

The Hackenthorpe Book of Lies

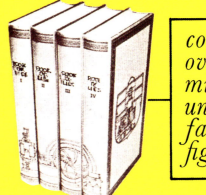

contains over 60 million untrue facts and figures.

* Did you know that the reason why windows steam up in cold weather is because of all the fish in the atmosphere?
* Did you know that Moslems are forbidden to eat glass?
* Did you know that the oldest rock in the world is the famous Hackenthorpe Rock, in North Ealing, which is 2 trillion years old?
* Did you know that Milton was a woman?
* Did you know that from the top of the Prudential Assurance Building in Bromley you can see 8 continents?
* Did you know that the highest point in the world is only 8 foot?

**** These are just a few of the totally inaccurate facts in **THE HACKENTHORPE BOOK OF LIES**

It's all in THE HACKENTHORPE BOOK OF LIES

A thorough and exhaustive source of misleading and untruthful information, compiled and edited by ex-Nobel Prizewinners Ron Hackenthorpe, Derek Hackenthorpe, Jeff 'The Nozz' Hackenthorpe and Luigi V. Hackenthorpe. There are 4 handsomely bound volumes, which can be purchased individually, or in our 'Pack Of Lies' gift set.

SLATER·METHUEN presents:

A monthly look at the world of ~~fish and~~ books.

The latest from Slater-Methuen: a Wonderful New Coffee-Table Book:

A Complete History of World Art and Everything Else By Eydie Gormé. An ideal coffee-table book. Comes complete with 4 attractive mahogany-style legs which screw into each corner of this beautifully produced art work. The cover is an exquisite detail from Caraveggio's 'Rape of Lucrece', covered in laminated plastic to withstand the most unpleasant stains.

Other Wonderful Bargains

The Complete Works of Virginia Woolf in high-quality asbestos. Line your fireplace with **Night and Day, Jacob's Room, To the Lighthouse.** Yes! This new edition of Virginia Woolf retains the heat all through the night.

At Last! A chance to wear one of England's greatest novels. The new flimsy nylon edition of **The Mayor of Casterbridge.** This exciting exploration of love, guilt and failure in 19th-century Dorchester can be worn as a nightie or as an eye-catching adornment to any cocktail or evening dress. You'll find all eyes on you when you wear **The Mayor of Casterbridge** (£4.95).

For the commercial traveller or the busy bachelor – **the Drip-dry edition of Dead Souls by Nicolai Gogol.** This great Russian novel can be washed through in the evening, hung in the bathroom overnight, and be clean *and* fresh in the morning. **Needs no ironing.**

Kids . . . shy, embarrassed . . .? Going through that difficult time when you think your face will never look lovely? Well, here, for you is *the Teen-Read Edition of the Rubaiyat of Omar Khayyam* complete with retractable hinged arm for dealing with facial problems. Tears off scabs, bursts pimples and rubs on Valderma while you are immersed in the exciting, mysterious world of Omar Khayyam.

For the discerning intellectual . . . the first **All Nude Version of Pride and Prejudice.** See Jane Austen's immortal characters in a variety of interesting positions. All nude!

Other Great Beaver Classics:

War and Peace: The Battle on the Ice—see everything!
The Ascent of F6: Derek and Nigel explore the kitchen-and each other!
Hard Times: Puts the Dick back in Dickens. Foreword by Rod Laver.

In next week's *Books and Book-men* ~~and hot Fish~~:

Barry Bucknell shows you how to make a bathroom extension from the works of Zola. **The Royal Signals Reading Champion** tells how he hopes to jump the **Complete works of G. K. Chesterton**—on a motor-bike! And **'Was Milton really batty?'**— a new and controversial look at the seventeenth-century poet and writer, by one of **Jacques Cousteau's** most trusted divers.

Some highlights from
MASTURBATORS OF HISTORY

new and forthcoming PYTHON LECTURES

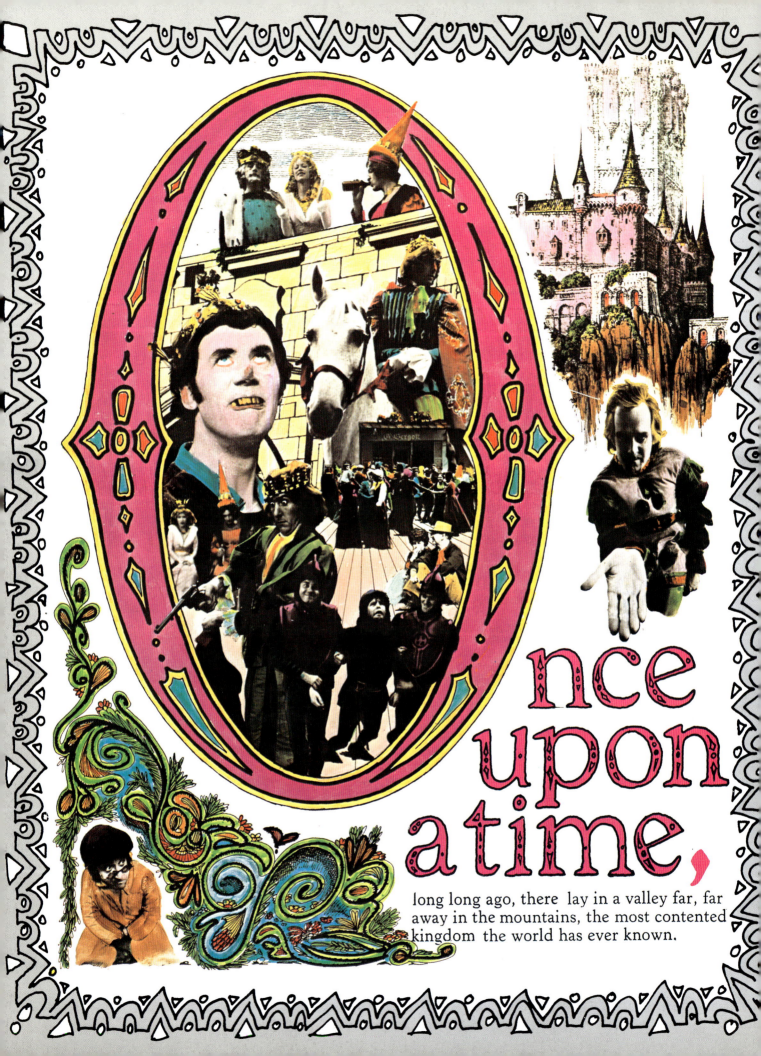

once upon a time,

long long ago, there lay in a valley far, far away in the mountains, the most contented kingdom the world has ever known.

It was called Happy Valley, and it was ruled over by a wise old King called Otto, and all his subjects flourished and were happy, and there were no discontents or grumblers, because Wise King Otto had had them all put to death along with the Trade Union leaders many years before. And all the good happy folk of Happy Valley sang and danced all day long, and anyone who was for any reason miserable or unhappy or who had any difficult personal problems was prosecuted under the Happiness Act.
(See, for example, R. *v.* Schlitz (1251). S, a carpenter, was heard moaning quietly contrary to Section 2 of the Cheerful Noises Act (1208); also admitted being depressed with malice aforethought under Section 1 of Happiness Act. Plea in mitigation that S's wife had died on previous day; S sentenced to be hanged by the neck until he cheered up.)

And, while the good people of Happy Valley tenaciously frolicked away, their wise old King, who was a merry old thing, played strange songs on his Hammond Organ up in the beautiful castle, where he lived with his gracious Queen Syllabub and their lovely daughter Mitzi Gaynor, who had fabulous tits and an enchanting smile, and wooden teeth which she bought in a chemist's in Augsberg, despite the fire-risk. She treasured these teeth which were made

of the finest pine and she varnished them after every meal. And next to her teeth her dearest love was her pet dog Hermann. She would take Hermann for long walks and pet and fuss over him all day long and steal him tasty titbits which he never ate, because sadly he was dead and no one had the heart to tell her because she was so sweet and innocent that she knew nothing of death or gastro-enteritis or even plastic hip joints. One day, while Mitzi was taking Hermann for a pull round the Royal Gardens, she set eyes on the most beautiful young man she had ever seen and fell head over heels in love with him, naturally assuming him to be a prince. Well, as luck would have it, he *was* a prince, and so, after looking him up in the *Observer's Book of Princes* to discover his name, she went and introduced herself and the subject of marriage, and, in what seemed like the twinkling of an eye, but was in fact a fortnight, they were on their way to see King Otto, to ask his permission to wed. What a perfect couple they looked! Mitzi, resplendent in a delicate shell-pink satin brocade and some new bullet-proof mahogany teeth, and Prince Kevin, handsome as could be, drawing many an admiring glance from some randy old closet queens in the vestibule.

Soon they were at the door of the Kingdom-Ruling Room. And then, trying to control their excitement, they were ushered into the presence of the King himself, who sat at the Royal State Organ singing his latest composition, the strangely discordant 'Ya bim dee bim, thwackety f'tang stirkel boo bum'. And when the King had finished, some hours later, and the courtiers' applause had died down, Mitzi presented Prince Kevin, who bowed gracefully and asked the wise old

King for his daughter's hand in marriage.

"Is he in the book?" asked the King.

"Oh yes, Daddy," cried Mitzi.

"And do you love my daughter?" he queried, penetratingly.

"I do, sir!" replied Prince Kevin, and a ripple of delight passed round the room for already Kevin's princely bearing and sweetness of nature had won the entire court's approval.

"Good! But first, before I can grant permission, I must set you a task that you may prove yourself worthy of my daughter's hand."

"I accept!!" cried Kevin gallantly.

The old King's face grew grave. "At nine o'clock tomorrow morning," he explained, "you must go to the top of the highest tower in this castle, and armed only with your sword, jump out of the window."

And so, early the next day, the brave young prince, dressed in a beautiful gold and white robe, and armed only with his magic sword, plummeted three hundred feet to a speedy death. How they all cheered! How funny the royal remains looked!

"Can we get married now, Daddy?" cried Mitzi, for as we know she knew nothing of death.

"No daughter, I'm afraid not," answered the wise old King, although he was himself a necrophilia buff, "he simply wasn't worthy of you."

"Oh dear," said Mitzi. "Will he have to go in the ground like all the others?"

And so most of Prince Kevin was buried alongside the remains of Prince Oswald (page 4 in the book) who'd had to fight an infantry division armed only with a copy of *The Guardian*; and Prince Robin (p. 19) who'd gallantly attempted to extinguish a fiery furnace by being thrown in it; and Prince Norbert (p. 36) who'd had to wrestle a combine harvester; and Prince Malcolm (p. 8) who'd had to catch a V.C.10, but had dropped it; and all the many other princes who'd been a touch unlucky in their quests.

So, the moment that Kevin's còffin had been laid to rest on the traditional huge black-edged Whoopee Cushion (for as Kevin was a prince, he had been granted a State Fancy Dress Funeral), Mitzi was off once again to the Royal Gardens, dragging the faithful Hermann behind her, to see if she could pull another prince. But alas, although most of the good folk of Happy Valley were there, the Carpenter and the Blacksmith and the Secret Policeman, and the Candlemaker and the Window-Dresser and his friend, and the Hangman and all his little apprentices, and the Writer-Performer and the Chartered Agent Provocateur, not a prince was to be seen. For princes had become extremely scarce; as rare, indeed, as an Australian virgin.

So Mitzi set off along the river bank, hopefully kissing frogs, until she was almost half-way to the Magic Scampi Provençale Bush when—all of a sudden! —she spotted the slightest glint of gold from beneath a Giggling Willow Tree and running forward, espied—sure enough!—a prince. He was rather thin and spotty, with a long nose, and bandy legs, and nasty unpolished plywood teeth, and a rare foot disease, but, thought Mitzi, a prince is a prince, and she fell in love with him without another thought.

And after a time, or a few times anyway, he, too, fell in love with her, and a few hours later they were on their way to ask wise King Otto's permission to wed, as this latest prince didn't read the newspapers any more than any of the others did, decadent, dimwitted, parasitic little bastards that they were.

ut as they made their happy way through the stately corridors that led to the Royal Chambers, by chance they came across Queen Syllabub being laid by a coloured gentleman.

"Heilo, Mummy," cried Mitzi, "this is Prince Walter."

"Hello, Prince Walter," cried Queen Syllabub graciously, slipping on her bra, "how nice to see you."

"Hello, Mummy's friend," cried Mitzi.

"Don't stare, darling," smiled the Queen, "this is Dr Erasmus, my new Algebra teacher."

"I guessed you were a doctor," cried Mitzi gaily, for she knew nothing of gynaecology. "Mummy, we're going to ask Daddy's permission to get married."

"Ah," muttered Queen Syllabub, "I want a word with him about that. I'll see you about the Binomial Theorem at eight o'clock, Doctor Erasmus."

"O.K. Queen," boomed her tinted mentor, "I'll bring the baby oil."

"Now Mitzi," continued our gracious Queen, hevelling herself, "is Walter kosher?"

"Page twenty," cried our sweet heroine, proffering the trusty tome. And then, "Does Daddy like Doctor Erasmus?"

"Best not to mention anything, darling," explained her mother. "Daddy's a little funny about darker people."

"I know nothing of racial prejudice," said Mitzi wistfully, for she knew nothing of racial prejudice.

"Now you two just wait here a moment," ordered Queen Syllabub, "I want a word with your father." And she strode forward into the Kingdom-Ruling Room, where, rudely interrupting the King's golden oldies ("Ni ni ni ni ni ni ni ni ni ni ni ni ni ni ni ni ni ni NI!!" 0001 on the HMV label) she explained in no uncertain terms that as Mitzi was rapidly running out of acceptable fiancés, Otto had better set this latest one an easy task or else.

s he in the book?" asked the King, surlily.

"Yes, Daddy," cried Princess Mitzi, delightedly.

"Do you love my daughter?" queried the wise old King.

"Could be," allowed Prince Walter,

3

nasally.

"Do you," continued the wise old King, "want her hand in marriage?"

An uneasy silence fell upon the assembled courtiers, for none of them much cared for Walter's looks, not even the Lord Chancellor, who was extremely gay.

". . . Yeah, all right."

"In that case," said the King, pursuing his line of thought most doggedly, for he knew full well that Queen Syllabub's first spouse had met with a mysterious end, "I must set you a task to prove you worthy of my daughter's hand."

"Why?" came the bold reply.

"Because she's a fuckin' Princess, that's why," explained the King, scarcely controlling his rage. "And your task is that you must, quite unaided and unarmed, go down the town and get me twenty Rothmans."

"What, now!?" exploded Walter.

"Not necessarily," cried the King weakly, smiling round the court with all the easy spontaneity of a chat show host, "I'll think about it."

ell, soon the day arrived when Prince Walter was to meet his challenge, in fact is was very soon, as it was the next day. The whole of Happy Valley gathered in the village square in great expectation. The King, Queen Syllabub and Princess Mitzi in all their finery sat on the gaily decorated scaffold surrounded by all the Royal Guards (except Brian Freud who was indisposed).

Suddenly the assembled throng fell silent as the commanding figure of Prince Walter slouched into the square and approached the royal party. With a few brief words the King stated Walter's task for all to hear, Queen Syllabub added the royal blessing and Princess Mitzi presented a pair of royal panties for him to carry on his quest as a token of her undying love and to ward off evil spirits.

With the tumultuous cheers of the excited crowd ringing in his ears, and the surge of the drum rolls echoing through the square, Walter, single-handed and armed only with half a pound, strode off on his quest. Yard after yard he walked, foot after foot, inch after inch, on and on, resolutely thrusting forward each leg in turn in the orthodox way, undeterred by the pebbles in the street and the birds flying overhead, on and on, and on and on, and on, ever forward, never looking back or at least not very often. Once perhaps, as Walter turned into Exceptional Crescent, the hordes of Happy Valley folk, and all the guests that had been invited from far and wide to witness the spectacle, and everyone else who had got tickets, sensed a moment's hesitation, a fleeting infirmity of purpose, as Walter seemed to falter, but it was only to scratch his crotch, and seconds later he was off again, beckoned ever forward by the glittering but forbidding prospect of the Splendido Tobacconist Shop just two doors down from the butcher's.

On and on he marched, pace upon pace, stride upon stride, until, at last, he stood before the portals of his Holy Grail, his improbable dream, his cherished target, as it were. The great shop lay before him!

A sudden stillness fell upon the crowds

clustering the pavements, thronging the windows of all the houses and inns and spilling over from all the tiny side streets. This was the moment of truth! It was now or not for a bit! Slowly Walter stepped towards the door, paused, gripped the doorknob and with one expert twist, turned it and thrust the door towards the tobacconist. The crowd gasped as he disappeared into the Splendido's murky depths.

Minutes passed. The crowd held their breath. Many fell unconscious as a result of this unintelligent behaviour. But then! The ring of a cash register! The sound of the doorknob turning and there was Walter! Standing victorious in the doorway, arm thrust proudly aloft and in his clenched fist—Yes! The 20 Rothmans, nestling effortlessly in their magnificent packet, the priceless cellophane glinting in the dazzling sunlight!!!

A joyous cry rang out throughout Happy Valley, and the crowds surged forward to salute the conqueror. Walter stood one moment, savouring the acclaim, and then, turning, started to retrace his steps, pace after pace, yard after yard, his feet alternating deftly, very much in the way already described when he was travelling in the opposite direction earlier. But not for long! For the rejoicing crowd, unable to contain themselves further, surged forward and sweeping their hero upwards, carried him shoulder high, back through Exceptional Crescent, into Anti-Depressant Street and round into the main square, setting him down in front of the royal platform just before the photograph was taken. How the square echoed and re-echoed with cheers! How thunderously the cymbals crashed! How joyously the old bells of the cathedral pealed forth! And as Walter proudly presented the fruits of his quest to King Otto, it almost seemed as though the birds on high filled the air with their purest rhapsodies while the flowers below opened their very blossoms in sweetest celebration.

"Where's my change?" queried the King.

"I've given it you," said Our Hero.

"I gave you ten bob," stated the King, for this was many many years before decimalisation. "How much were they?"

"Shut your gob, Otto," muttered the Queen, waving graciously. "And give him Mitzi's hand."

"Halt!" cried a mysterious voice, lilting and musical, yet strangely strong and masculine, like an inspired newsreader.

All eyes in the square swivelled to the source of the voice described in the line above and lo! There before them, astride a magnificent Arab stallion, sat a princely figure, more beautiful than Apollo, more commanding even than Richard Attenborough, more royal than the Duke of Kent himself.

"Halt I prithee!" cried this apotheosis of young manhood. "Gentle King, pray halt!"

"Who are you?" demanded King Otto, quite bewildered.

"I am Prince Charming of the Kingdom of the Golden Lakes," cried the god-like creature, as his attendants

5

wheeled the magnificent stallion forward. "Page five in The Book. And I claim the hand of your beautiful daughter Princess Mitzi!"

A gasp of astonishment rose from the village square.

"You're too late," shouted Prince Walter.

"What?" cried the butch vision.

"I got her, Charming," snarled our former hero, "now buzz off!"

"Wait a minute!" The Queen was on her feet. "Mitzi is not betrothed yet!"

"What?" screamed Prince Walter. "The King said if I got him twenty Rothmans I could 'ave her."

"Got him *twenty Rothmans*?" repeated Prince Charming, in astonishment.

"I had to go into the town."

"For this priceless treasure," cried the gallant Prince Charming, indicating the beautiful Mitzi Gaynor, who had risen to her feet and was now eyeing this golden princeling with something approaching pure lust. "For this most perfect of God's creatures, for this finest and most delicate flower in the whole of this geographical area, I will face in mortal combat, that most dreaded of all creatures . . ."

"An emu!!" gasped the crowd.

"No, no, no," cried Prince Charming. "A dragon!"

"We accept," cried the Queen.

"We accept," cheered the villagers, to a man, or to a woman, as the case may have been.

"Where's he going to get a dragon from?" squealed Prince Walter.

Prince Charming favoured him with a gracious smile.

"I provide my own."

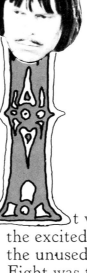

t was a beautiful Spring morning, the excited crowds were milling around the unused dog track where the Dragon Fight was to take place. Hermann had died, you see, the day before the dog track was opened, and as Mitzi had registered Hermann as an entry in all the races, and as he would have run last (on account of his being dead) and as r oyal pets must not fail, under the Constitution of Happy Valley the races were cancelled; but as Mitzi continued to enter Hermann whenever new races were announced, these races too were always being cancelled at the last minute. (Due to expected rain.) This had been going on in Happy Valley for over six years. The Editor says this is not relevant but I wanted you to know anyway, just for background.

Anyway . . . everyone was there, clustered round the edge of the specially erected ring, jostling for the best views, chattering excitedly, and laughing merrily at the antics of some of the high-spirited youths who had clambered into the arena and were now roasting an immigrant, on a spit wittily improvised from a flagpole borrowed from the Royal Stand. Suddenly an outburst of ironic cheering and cat-calls announced that the Royal Family were taking their places in their Special Box, King Otto leading the way playing selections from Bizet on his new Japanese wrist organ, Mitzi close behind accompanied by the Lord Chancellor, then Queen Syllabub and Archduke Harry, the Lord Chief Justice and the Archbishop, and Field Marshal Spratbanger and Admiral Spam-Willoughby-Spam, followed by all the courtiers and attendants carrying the ceremonial crates of brown ale and cheese and onion rolls. Soon they had reached their places, and they stood a few moments waving to the crowd while the Lord Chancellor argued about the tickets with the Royal Usherette. Then they were seated, and, almost immediately, a great cheer erupted from the crowd as it espied the heart-quickening figure of Prince Charming and his fine stallion being wheeled into the arena. Excited applause broke out and a chant of, "Char-ming . . . Char-ming . . . Char-ming" on the Kop was taken up by the record 22,407 crowd (with the single exception of Prince Walter, sitting in the middle of the East Stand sporting a Dragon rosette, who whistled derisively and apprehensively picked his nose with great abandon).

Prince Charming halted, and paused a moment, his golden hair reflecting the rays of the sun and his broad, manly shoulders visibly expanding in the heat, while his attendants moved the ladder into position, and then, gracefully, delicately, firmly, confidently, tenaciously, boldly, deftly, commandingly, irrefutably, yet poignantly, he descended, and bowed low in the direction of the royal box. At this very moment, there rang out over the arena the most terrifying roar, the most utterly blood-curdling bellow that Happy Valley had heard in a thousand years. It was, to make no bones about it, bloody loud, about 12,000 watts at a guess, and it was a sound of such indescribable strangeness, that it cannot be described.

The crowd, quaking and trembling, shrank back in sheer horror and awestruck, stared aghast in the direction of the huge pantechnicon drawn up at the edge of the ring. A second hideous screech followed the first and before the crowd could even gasp, the side of the pantechnicon fell open revealing to their awe-struck gaze . . . the dragon !!! A single sheet of solid flame flashed forth and with one bound, the fearsome creature sprang into the ring, baying a third grotesque, spine-chilling shriek. Even Prince Charming, for one fleeting moment, seemed frozen by this appalling sight and from the East Stand floated Walter's solitary chant . . . "Ea-sy, Ea-sy!"

For a second the dragon stood poised as though bemused by his surroundings. Charming measured his frightful adversary. As its massive jaws gaped he could see the red-hot tongue flicking viciously inside, the glitter of the razor-edged teeth, the foul sacs of venom hanging from the armoured neck, the macabre ears, the baleful blood-shot eyes, and the positively alarming hairs up its nose. And what a ferociously shaped body!! Spiked ribs of poisonous thorns ringed its scaly slimy back, and great ironclad plates clustered round its private parts. Its feet were pretty frightening too. And as for its tail! It had a curl in it that would have put the wind up Mohammed Ali. The whole ghastly nightmarish beast could not have been an inch less than one foot long and in height nearly as high as a rabbit.

Charming's jaw tightened. With one thrust of his golden shoe he was on his way toward the dragon, moving lightly across the sun-dried sand, cautious yet determined, with all the smooth power of a panther, the poise of a matador, and the grace of God. Still the dragon waited, roaring hideously into its throat-mike and breathing great jets of flame three eighths of an inch long. Thirty feet, twenty feet . . . ten feet! The tension was at breaking point! Five feet . . . four . . . three . . . Charming checked his stride for one brief moment, a single bead of fear glistening on his brow and then, as the dragon drew back its head to charge, he drew his trusty Luger and blew its tiny brains out.

"Foul!!!", cried Walter, but his appeal was swallowed up in the thunderclap of emotion that greeted this mighty feat! How the arena echoed and re-echoed with cheers! How thunderously . . . (see page 5 for further details). And so Prince Charming and Mitzi were married that very afternoon and went to live at the Royal Palace of the Kingdom of the Golden Lakes with King and Queen Charming, and when King Charming died they took over the Royal Toy Dragon farm and bred many new varieties and made a packet and lived happily ever after. And Walter soon got over it, and settled down, and became an accountant and did very well for himself, really, and married a very very nice girl, a little plain some people said but very nice, and bought a second-hand Rover and a little house in Watford. They had a little boat too and they used to go to Majorca for their holidays. Walter often suggested going to Happy Valley instead but Brenda felt they wouldn't really fit in there now so they never did.

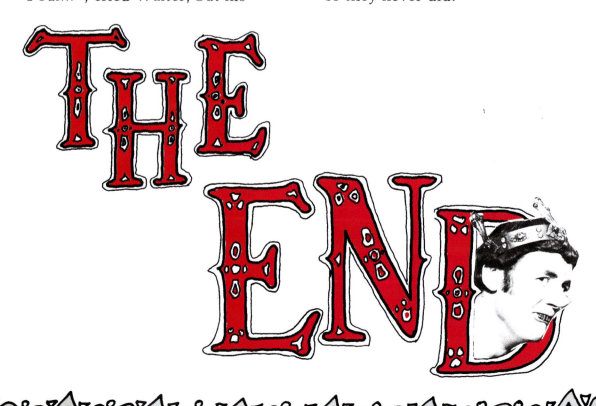

THE END

Ferndean School Report

Report for **Spring Jan 17th — April 20th** Term 19**73**

Name **God**   Form **V**

Subject	Exam Marks %	Master's Comments	
English	11	Poor, Handwriting weak	RP
French	9	Very Poor	AJ
Geography	30	Swimmingly poor. His knowledge appears somewhat dated. Interesting ideas about rock formation. Keeps going "Kerpow!"	EMVS
Biology	28	Weak: thinks he knows it all. Constantly rude about Darwin	
Divinity	14	Poor. Keeps disputing Biblical facts. He refuses to read the bible on the grounds that he was "misquoted."	Rev. Hall
Latin	100	Quite the best scholar I've ever had.	J.B
Woodwork	87	An excellent Carpenter. Mary & I are still very fond of him	
Domestic Science	54	A useful little cook. The pillar of salt will come in handy for a dry time. Mrs Yates	
Art	62	Very creative. However he does keep claiming to have created everything including myself Mr Vidler, the organist, & even several Town Boys.	
Games		Will not row. Hates games and once parted the waters of the swimming pool during a match against the old boys, which was both unsporting & dangerous. He can still do press-ups. Ron Bright (games master)	

Progress and Conduct   I'm afraid that I am severely disappointed in God's works. All three of him have shown no tendency to improve and He merely sits at the back of the class talking to himselves. He has shown no interest in Rugger, asked to be excused Prayers, and moves in a mysterious way. What is more his omnipresence is beginning to cause some embarrassment in big school, since he is continually out of bounds, and of course at the same time always in Matron's bed. Finally his attentions to the carpentry master's fiancée caused her to leave a term early and there are several nasty rumours flying about the house.   Mr. C. Alverson.   **Form Master**

Housemaster's Remarks   I am very sorry to be losing God's ability + friendliness from the house. We will never forget how He made the Model Railway Club layout in six days! It seems unlikely he will now get into Oxford or Cambridge, but I could recommend him for a job with I.C.I. or Unilever   Eric Pope   **Housemaster**

Combined Cadet Force

They were a very promising Lance Corporal, and showed particular interest in the L.M.G and weapon training.

Captain Curran C.O.   **Divinity Master**

Next term will begin on **6th May** and end on **17th July.**   **Head Master**

100th YEAR

FRI ... APRIL 20

BARGAINS
DIAMOND
RINGS—£10-1000

The Stratton Indicator

No. 8104

3 pence

SOME OPPOSITION TO LOCAL LAY-BY SCHEME

COUNCILLORS were divided today on their attitude to the proposed new scheme to place a modern lay-by on the old B529 Stratton-Hoo Road.

Accidents

It was felt by many that such a scheme could cause a steep rise in accidents on the B529, hitherto one of the most accident-free roads in the area. 'We haven't had a crash here for fifty years' said local resident Ivan Pigg. 'In fact we haven't had a car here for ten.' Residents plan to boycott the £20 lay-by when it is built. Feelings about the lay-by ran high at a public meeting when the designer of the scheme Laurence Whelk faced his critics. 'We must keep in line with modern thinking' he argued, 'there is no lay-by on the B529 from Alderstown to Stanshall, a distance of five and a half miles.'

Survey

A local survey, he claimed, had revealed the need for such a scheme. This was denied by residents whc

produced the results of their own survey which showed that within a typical twenty-four year period only seven

vehicles had used the B529.

The debate continues, See Pages 32-47 inside.

Stratton go top of the League

By defeating arch-rivals neighbouring Cubsy by one run on Saturday Stratton go top of the Grisdale League, two points ahead of Sudsy and Wells. The main feature of their victory was a superb

innings by local man skipper Hemsley who held off the Cubsy bowlers when the match seemed to be swinging their way. Details of the Match

Cubsy

Groat c. & b. Wilkes	0
Sprange l.b.w., b. Wilkes	0
Thompson J. run out	1
Caryotid P. st. Si, b. Rant	0
Flake c. Limp, b. Wilkes	0
Tickersley not out	0
Watt J. l.b.w., b. Rant	0
Armstrong B. c. Rotter, b. Wilkes	0
Fletcher N. b. Rant	0
Thompson E. ht. wkt, b. Parkes	0
Extras	—
Total—All Out	1

Stratton

Parkes b. Thompson	0
Si c. & b. Caryotid	0
Rant P. not out	1
Rotter b. Thompson	0
Limp rtd. hurt	0
Wilkes c. Watt, b. Caryotid	0
Cooke C. l.b.w., b. Watt	0
Cook P. b. Caryotid	0
Sampson R. st. Flake, b. Groat	0
Hemsley not out	0
Extras	—
Total for nine	1

Accident at Stratton Black Spot

The third accident in twelve years occurred at Barnley crossing yesterday when Mr Ron Stig was involved in a collision with a stationary

a bus was coming, he wouldn't be alive today,' said Mrs Elsie Which. 'He is a very lucky man.'

Misprint: An Apology

We apologise for a misprint in our last edition. It should have read 'Misprint; Ad Apology' and not 'Mispring: An apology.' Sory.

L-Driver in severe parking offence

Derek K. Birdsall of McGoering Terrace, Rendham, was today severely fined for his part in what police called "wilful and persistently evil parking'. The defendant pleaded guilty and was fined £5 with £1 costs. He said in his defence that he couldn't find a kosher car park.

	0
	0
	0
	0
	0
	2
	—
	2

President Nixon to visit Stratton

In our last edition the headline 'President Nixon to Visit Stratton, should have read 'President Dixon to visit Stratton'. This refers to the visit of Wilfred Dixon, President of the Harmsworth Film Society who gave an interesting talk on symbolism in the early Pet Clark films.

wall. 'It was a miraculous escape,' said one eye-witness, 'he fell off his bicycle and just missed rolling on to the busy Stratton by-pass four miles away.' 'Had this happened on a main road whilst

Angry residents demanded a motorway should be built on the spot 'with no speed limits.' 'We are sick and tired of waiting around here all day for accidents,' said a group of mothers.

Proposed bus route unlikely to affect School children says Blueways Spokesman

A Spokesman for 'Blueways' said that the proposed new

bus route was unlikely to affect schoolchildren.

Drugs Charge

A man was in remand today accused of possessing nearly 1,000 bottles of Aspirin. Mr Arthur Martin, age 40, described as a chemist was remanded. It was said in court that he told the police that he sold the aspirin for a living. 'We simply don't believe him' said a Detective.

WORLD NEWS IN BRIEF

Famine in Africa causes thousands to die

Earthquake in Europe reported

British PM shot in sailing accident

America to scrap elections

Germany re-united

War declared

LOCAL FILMS

Geraldo Cinema, Oliver Reed in 'The Chauvinists'.

TOWN HALL REBUILDING FUND

The town hall rebuilding fund has now reached £568,000,000. It is the largest single privately administered fund in Western Europe. The Lord Mayor of Stratton warned against complacency, however.

Press on

'I shall press on' said Mr Whim to journalists. 'I intend to convince the Council that they are wrong. This garden shed is going to be built, and when they see the Architect's presents I'm sure they will change their minds.' Mr Whim is head of a large road haulage firm and building works and has had many successful contracts with the Council.

Stratton Green a new seat

The Stratton U.D.C. decided by a vote of 1-0 last week, to go ahead with preliminary work on clearing a site for the construction of a wooden seat opposite the chemists. The seat will face slightly North-West and be constructed of reinforced plywood with a teak veneer. Its 4 legs will be free-standing on a concrete base. It replaces the old seat demolished when police mistakenly opened fire on a group of schoolchildren last summer, killing 8 and damaging the woodwork irretrievably.

Permission to build new garden shed refused

Mr Leonard Whim (39), a local man, today attacked the decision of the Town Borough Council to refuse him permission to construct another garden shed near his £10,000 house in lower Ching, on the grounds that he already had one shed. 'This is worse than living in a communist state' Mr Leonard told one of our reporters. 'To my mind it's creeping socialism. I fought in the war for freedom to build garden sheds when and where you wanted.

Mrs Whim, 32, a trim, petite, blonde wearing a matching tweed costume in striking aquamarine with elegant lace-up boots, and a fiery rose hat, agreed, said a neighbour. Leonard Whim is well-known in the area and has two dogs.

A Councillor defended the

unhappy about Mr Whim's plans to build a box-girder garden shed with split-level shopping piazza, covered walk-way, underground garage-cum-swimming pool, with facilities for all-night split-level shopping, and a split-level entertainment centre complete with bowling alley and split-level bingo hall.

decision amidst angry scenes outside the 17th Century 'Clatch', which is shortly to be demolished to make way for a new car-park. 'This whole thing' he said 'has been blown up out of all proportion. Although one or two members of the Council were quite frankly a little

BIRTHS, MARRIAGES AND DARTS

BIRTHS

Follicle: To Renee and Ken Follicle, a son, Walter Moulson. To Jennie Moulson and Ken Follicle, a son, Eddie
Rogers: To Irene Rogers and Ken Follicle, a son, Frank.

MARRIAGES

Gort-Follicle: The marriage took place on Saturday of Judy, youngest daughter of Colonel Victor Gort of 'the Kaffirs', Reichstag Road, Stratton, and Ken Follicle. The bride wore a jasmine

dress with a tunic front, white lace ribbons and a matching bouquet of early primroses. Mr Follicle wore a dressing gown and slippers. The reception was held at the Dirty Rabbit.

DARTS

The Darts Match between the Dirty Rabbit and the Fox and Gynaecologist, resulted in a dramatic win for the Fox and Gynaecologist. The match was lost in the very last throw when the captain of the visitors, needing only a double 4 to win, ran amok through the village, pillaging, raping and burning people's houses.

Stratton must move with the times, says Lord Mayor

'Stratton must move with the times' said the Lord Mayor last week.

Play Cheeseshop

An exciting new Word Game for Two based on Real Life Retailing

The rules are simple:

1. The two players write down the names of as many Nineteenth-Century British Prime Ministers as they can remember.
2. Whoever remembers the least is the Victim, or Customer.
3. The other is the Prankster or Shopkeeper.
4. The Victim next asks the Shopkeeper for a type of cheese.
5. The Shopkeeper, who has no cheese whatsoever in his shop, must then give an excuse why he does not have that particular variety. If he simply says that he does not have it he loses the game. He must give an excuse (see below for a few examples).
6. The Victim then asks for another variety of cheese.
7. The Shopkeeper gives another excuse.
8. This continues until either:
   (a) the Customer runs out of new names of varieties of cheeses *or* repeats himself, in which case the **Shopkeeper wins;** or
   (b) the Shopkeeper keeps the Customer in his shop for three minutes, in which case the **Shopkeeper wins;** or
   (c) the Customer attacks the Shopkeeper or has a fit of any kind, in which case the **Shopkeeper wins;** or
   (d) the Shopkeeper pauses for more than three seconds before giving an excuse *or* repeats himself, in which case the **Customer wins** (this is not like real life, but then this is a game); or
   (e) the Shopkeeper admits he has no cheese at all, in which case the **Customer wins** and may punch the **Shopkeeper** in the teeth.

Special long version of game for real life shopkeepers:

Rules are the same but the Customer must be kept in the shop for forty minutes.

A few simple excuses for beginners:

1. There's very little call for it around here.
2. The van was supposed to be bringing it in this morning.
3. We never have it on Wednesday.
4. We would stock it but it goes off so quickly.
5. It's very seldom sold these days.
6. It'll be in tomorrow.
7. I wouldn't recommend that one really.
8. We just sold the last piece.
9. I'll have a look. . . . I'm sorry the cat must have had it.
10. May I ask what you're eating it *with*?
11. Shall I order some for you?
12. We're fresh out of it.
13. It's a bit too runny, I wouldn't want to sell it to you like this.
14. Taylor's down the road might have some.
15. There's been a run on it this week.
16. We haven't got that as such.

For lactophobes the following variations are recommended:

Fish-shop
Book-shop or Library
Pet-shop
Greengrocer

The National Institute of Historical Research *(Founded 1973)* Proudly Announces

The Official Medallic Commemoration of the History of Mankind

The vital, dramatic and very fascinating history of Man himself, which will be of particular interest to all human beings, is now to be made official, by the issue of these fine medallions, with nice pictures on them, and not too many words.

ABSOLUTELY FREE!

Hallmarked First Edition Proof Sets in solid Welsh Silver* are available ONLY by advance covenanted subscription or, of course, cash. To preserve value, the number of sets minted must be strictly limited to the number we can actually sell. No more will be minted after this number is reached, in order to guarantee rarity.

* A very attractive and valuable Zinc/Bakelite alloy

This Magnificent Set of Shiny Bright Objects will be of particular interest, not only to everyone, but especially to Collectors of Objets d'Art and Jackdaws.

All Hallmarked First Edition Proof Sets are clearly marked 'Hallmarked First Edition Proof Set' to distinguish them from Non-Hallmarked First Edition Proof Sets, and Hallmarked Second (or Third) Edition Proof Sets, and Hallmarked First Edition Non-Proof Sets, none of which exists. However the words 'Hallmarked First Edition' and 'Proof' have associations with objects of value and so are clearly marked on these medallions.

Mrs René Descartes sleeping

Edward the Confessor at a loose end

Napoleon forging luncheon vouchers

Jack Hobbs stabbed in his bath by Charlotte Rampling

Marie Curie eludes Nero's troops by hiding in a lift

Leonardo da Vinci nearly inventing Canasta

Peter the Great carving his initials on a passing vicar

George Washington shortly before intercourse with Mary Baker Eddy

Oliver Cromwell in Stand by Your Bedouin *with Brian Rix*

The medallions, which are definitely Collector's Items, have been designed by Arthur Penn, F.R.H.S. (aged 12) and will be minted by Quick, Turn and Partners of Old Bond Street. They will come complete with a Superb Presentation Cardboard Box specially designed by Arthur Penn for keeping them in. This beautiful box with your own name specially written on the lid in ink, contains a superbly roneoed sheet of paper with all the Relevant Facts about World History on it, and has been specially designed to hold all the magnificent medallions, but also to fit easily into the Specially Designed Cupboard Under Your Stairs when everyone's had a quick look at them.

THE ANA~GRAMS GAPE (4)

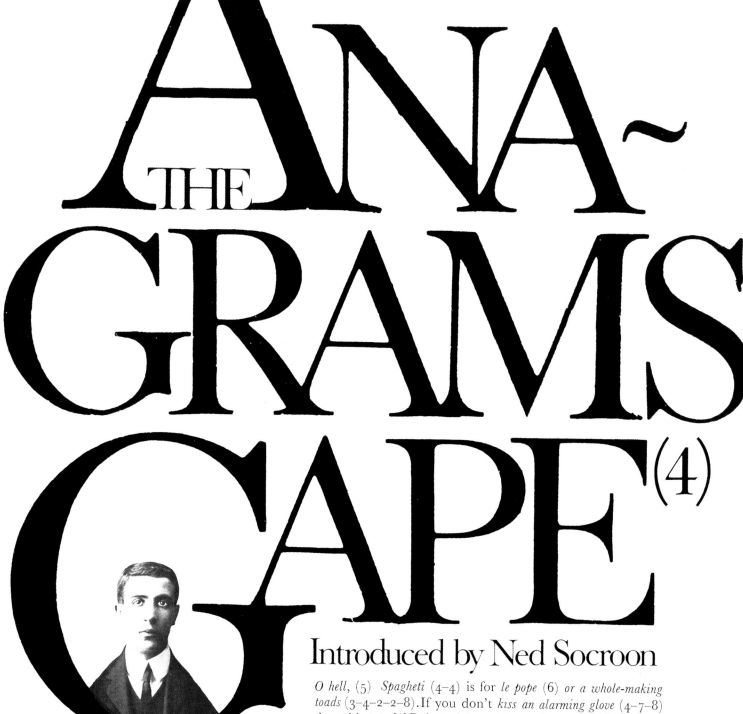

Introduced by Ned Socroon

O hell, (5) *Spagheti* (4–4) is for *le pope* (6) *or a whole-making toads* (3-4-2-2-8). If you don't *kiss an alarming glove* (4–7–8) then this *type WE tin penis* (4-3-7) is not for you. In fact if you don't *kill AA, strangle a Ma* (4–8–2–3) then you probably won't even *hear Dave* (4–4) this far, and only those who *are marginally leaks* (6–4–8) will be *felt* (4). So to all those who do *vole* (4) anagrams, a very *glib hole* (3–5) and a *wee calm worm* (4–7). *God fund* (4–3) aren't they? Much better than *or bold gin* (6–3) sex, putting your *an sty* (5) where it shouldn't be. No, give *rams a mange* (2–8) any day, far better than *dude i.e. snob* (4–6) rubbing against *soft flaked hens* (5–5). Well, *yeb-yeb* (3–3) and keep up the good *krow* (4)

Yours *secrinely* (9)
Ron Coondes (3–7)

Solution to Anagrams page
(O get an orgasm Lou, I pants. a!! (8–2–8–4))

Hello. This page is for people who like to do anagrams. If you don't like solving anagrams then this tiny wee snippet is not for you, in fact if you don't like anagrams at all then you probably won't even have read this far, and only those who really like anagrams will be left. So to all those who do love anagrams a very big hello and a warm welcome. Good fun aren't they? I really love them much better than boring old sex, putting your nasty where it shouldn't be. No, give me anagrams any day, far better than nude bodies rubbing against soft naked flesh. Well bye-bye and keep up the good work.

Yours sincerely,
Des O'Connor

Hello, and welcome to a page written entirely for people who dislike anagrams. Hi, anagram-haters everywhere! Down with all words or phrases formed with the letters of another! This page is specially dedicated to all who hate and despise the pathetic practice of shuffling letters to form different meanings. Let us make one thing clear from the start, there will be no anagrams on this page at all. None whatsoever. So any anagram lovers can just turn to their own page, where they will find their pathetic practice sufficiently catered for. We want none of you here. For too long we anti-anagrammatists have had to put up with the smugness of those who possess the reprehensible ability to perceive concealed meanings hidden in words or phrases. Now no more; this page is guaranteed free from anagrams. So just you put your feet up and relax without worrying whether you are reading concealed anagrams or not. Don't you just hate those bores who can crack an anagram faster than they can pour the irate? I'm sorry. That wasn't an anagram. It was a typing error. It should of course have read 'I rate her pout'. Oh dear. I'm sorry again. That wasn't a typing error. It was a printer's slip. The phrase 'heat our tripe' should have read 'I rape her tout'. Oh golly. Sorry. I'm afraid that owing to a mistake in the proof-reading the phrase 'rip her eat out' has been wrongly corrected to 'ripe teat hour'. It should of course have read 'at trip out here'. Oh crikey. I'm terribly sorry but the phrase 'our pi theatre' which we wrongly informed you was 'the route pair' should have been printed 'rather I toupé' and not 'ripe hate tour'. Oh no. Drat the bally thing. I'm most frightfully sorry but the phrase 'Report the A.U.I.' has been wrongly given as 'therapeutior', when it should quite obviously have read 'opiate hurter'.

Anagrams – A statement

It looks very much as though this page written especially for people who dislike anagrams has been sabotaged. It appears that someone has infiltrated the text at a crucial stage and tampered with the words, so that certain phrases have been red teal (7). We apologise to all haters of anagrams for the annoyance and inconvenience. It's all very ira tit gin r (10). But there you ear (3). What can neo od? (3–2). We are taking legal pests (5) to tup (3) the matter right but until then we can only loose a pig (9). The Tiredo (6).

An announcement

Because of the Anagrams dispute it has been decided to devote the rest of this space to a page specially written for people who like figures of speech, for the not a few fans of litotes and those with no small interest in meiosis, for the infinite millions of hyperbole-lovers, for those fond of hypallage and the epithet's golden transfer, for those who fall willingly into the arms of the metaphor, those who give up the ghost, bury their heads in the sand and ride roughshod over the mixed metaphor, and even those of hyperbaton the friends. It will be too, for those who reprehend the malapropism; who love the wealth of metonymy; for all friends of rhetoric and syllepsis; and zeugmatists with smiling eyes and hearts. It will bring a large absence of unsatisfactory malevolence to periphrastic fans; a wig harm bello to spoonerists; and in no small measure a not less than splendid greeting to you circumlocutors. The World adores prosopopeiasts, and the friendly faces of synechdochists, and can one not make those amorous of anacoluthon understand that if they are not satisfied by this, what is to happen to them? It will attempt to really welcome all splitters of infinitives, all who are Romeo and Juliet to antonomasia, those who drink up similes like sparkling champagne, who lose nothing compared with comparison heads, self-evident axiomists, all pithy aphorists, apothegemists, maximiles, theorists, epigrammatists and even gnomists. And as for the lovers of aposiopesis – ! It will wish bienvenu to all classical adherents of euphuism, all metathesistic birds, golden paronomasiasts covered in guilt, fallacious paralogists, trophists, anagogists, and anaphorists; to greet, welcome, embrace asyndeton buffs, while the lovers of ellipsis will be well-met and its followers embraced, as will be chronic worshippers of catachresis and supporters of anastrophe the world over.

Another announcement

Hello. There appears to have been some difficulty in getting the Page for People who are Fond of Figures of Speech started, so it has been abandoned. Owing to shortage of space we're going to continue on this page with the special page for readers who are interested in foundation garments, leatherware and split-crotch panties. *Hello all foundation, leather and split-crotch buffs, what a year it's been, eh? With lingerie getting naughtier and more inventive by the day one can hardly keep abreast of it. If you're into foundation garments then the new* Regina, *without unnecessary straps and hurtful buckles, will be for you. (It's also available with the unnecessary straps – and hurtful buckles, extra.) Likewise there's a new combination truss and panti-hose supporter in – yes – leather, or you can buy it in the cheaper vinyls and PVC. Split-crotch panties have taken a giant step for Man into the Space Age of Naughty Underwear with the Buzz Aldrin Briefs, which open up easily for* **I'm sorry to butt in like this, but I'm the Editor and I'd like to apologize for the cluttered and messy appearance of this page. This is due not only to the lateness of delivery of material, but I'm afraid I must say this, a certain amount of bickering amongst the writers. If I may say so without appearing bitchy, one or two little overbloated egos have been at work, certain precious little writers who think they're bloody Hermann Hesse instead of jumped-up overpaid television scriptwriters who got lucky** *revealing at the crucial point where they part the face of Buzz Aldrin himself. If you now paste down the edges of the sailor's uniform until the word 'Maudling' is almost totally obscured* **Hello. I'm a friend of the Editor's and I want just to say how sorry I am that he's got himself into a bit of a mess over this page. Perhaps he took on too much with this book, but it was the glamour and romance of publishing which drew him to it. He thought he'd get the pick of the girls, he thought he'd be surrounded by the Eyre Methuen groupies, he thought he'd wine and dine with the real Princess Margaret and be inundated with invitations to all-night champagne parties with Christina Foyle. Alas the harsh realities of modern publishing were too much for a man of his sensitivity. Perhaps sensitivity is too kind a word for his particular weakness, perhaps incompetence would be closer to it. In any case I for one never thought he was right for the job. There were many of us just as talented, if not more so, who could quite easily have been Editor if only we'd been asked, and would probably have made a much better job of editing without half the prima donna fuss she's made about it love. Bitch bitch bitch all day long, and look what she's got for it, a right bloody shambles. Well this is one scrape she can get herself out of** *and there's plenty of room for one, or even two melons inside, if you wish.*

Throughout the difficult years of the 30's, when the lessons of Versailles were being all too bitterly learnt, when the international economic situation . . . tottered from crisis to crisis, I was busy tarting up Ramsay's barnet, and Ramsay's sitting there looking through the *Sporting Chronicle* when he says, 'Hey Mervyn, wot are you?'. Well I think to meself, 'allo . . . he's sussed me,' so I says, 'All right, so what, yes I'm gay'. But Ramsay says 'No wot star are you?' . . . and you know I don't think he ever caught on that I was bent — which was just as well, 'cos he was a right gent and a good customer. I don't care what people say about him splitting the Labour party, he looked great with a D.A. and quiff.

- BY STANLEY BALDWIN'S LANDLADY -

your stars

The only Horoscope to correctly foretell the outcome of the Tottenham– Margate Cup Tie in 1973, and to be nearly right about Haile Selassie. This horoscope is compiled by careful study of the movements of the stellar universe, it's not just bloody guessing. INTRODUCTION BY RAMSAY MACDONALD'S HAIRDRESSER

32% holding in Pisces through his own company Charles Forte (World Domination) Ltd.

NORMAN MAILER: A new sign, with every prospect of a very good year indeed.

GLC: Another new sign, but I'm afraid a very disappointing one. People born under the GLC will have a very cramped year.

LEO: A nice old one. Please do not feed it buns and things.

SCORPIO: Scorpions are masty things which should be stamped on. Prediction: Jan.–March: You will be stamped on. April–Aug: You will be stamped on. Sept. onwards: You will be stamped on again.

MOLLY PARKIN: A very rare sign. You will probably continue to work in journalism.

VIRGO: You will be thoroughly mocked by boring people in pubs every time you mention that you are a Virgo. Change your sign. Try Harrods — a good year.

SLATER–LIBRA: A new and rapidly expanding starsign formed last year with the take-over of Cancer Holdings Ltd, Gemini Property Signs and Libra. The only starsign with a properly balanced portfolio and regular dividends, but liable to Capital Gains Tax. Avoid discussions of morality.

AQUARIUS: Aquarians have one thing in common — hip injuries. So avoid any activities which may involve strain on the hip. This includes opium eating and pushing heavy pianos with your hip. However, if despite all precautions you *do* sustain a hip injury, then hop along to the Hip Centre in Leicester . . . but for heaven's sake travel outside rush hour because there is an 80–60 chance of sustaining further hip injuries from people jostling, pushing and rubbing their hips up against yours. Don't, for heaven's sake, be one of those people who hate to make a fuss. If you feel pressure on your hip, that is

aggravating the injury, don't be afraid to say 'Excuse me, I have a hip injury, which you are exacerbating'. This will relieve the pressure on the hip, and could well mean the difference between restoration of your existing hip, and the fitting of a totally new hip — either a Wellington Handyhip or the Datsun motorised hip and radio.

HARRODS: This is quite the best sign, and certainly the most expensive. It'll be a very good year for the Music Department, perhaps wedding bells for the Food Hall during August, and the Gift Department may go through

a difficult time with a Married Man in October. The only drawback of this sign is that it is closed weekends.

ARIES: This sign may well be cancelled next year.

DERRY AND TOM'S: It will be an exciting year for you; apart from the mass rape you will be run over twice, and eaten by a boa constrictor. Apart from the rape, it's worth changing to another star.

SAGITTARIUS: The only Zodiacal sign owned by the Trust-House Forte group, though Charles Forte has a

---

your letters
By AC/DC

Since reading your magazine I have stopped wearing knickers. P. P. de Grenouille, Aix-en-Provence
Dear Ed, While reading your magazine I have **started** wearing knickers   J. Lloyd **Cheltenham**
Talk about spanking! My wife and I were on holiday a couple of years ago and we met this extremely nice couple who holidayed in Ibiza every year. One evening we'd all had a little too much to drink, it was a very warm night and they suggested that we all went down to the beach for a midnight dip. Unfortunately my husband and I had no swimming costumes with us, so we

couldn't go. Yours, 'Naughty' of Hastings
Our resident psychiatrist writes: *I am their resident psychia trist.*
Arthur Resident Psychiatrist
Dear Guys,
I am extremely rich and work for another sex magazine. Do you think you could get me some girls?   Victor III
Our resident fag writes:
Victor sweetheart what you need is someone who'll understand you and take care of you, Not just a woman, but how real men feel. Why not give me a buzz and give it a

whirl? You've nothing to lose
When I first read your magazine I stopped wearing a bra. Now since reading J.C.'s letter 'How to drive men mad' I have stopped wearing panties as well,
Yours sincerely,
The Reverend Milton Randall
Dear Folks,
Since reading your magazine I have stopped wearing glasses. Will it really make me blind?   Ron Hiccough
Our resident expert writes:
Regular reading of this magazine will NOT make you

blind. Only very very stupid.
Dear Ed,
Some people say that all your letters are made up by the people who write your magazine. In that case is this letter also written by the people who write your magazine?   Yours, Ed.
The Editor writes:
All our letters are genuinely written and sent in by the public. If you do not believe us come round here any time and we will be prepared to show you conclusive violence.
Dear Ed, I wanted to tell you how much I am enjoying your magazine. Please excuse shaky handwriting.
Yours Anne Old-Joak

Hamsters: A Warning

Hello, I'd like to have a word with you about a problem that many people, like yourself, are probably unaware of.

I'm talking, of course, about hamsters.

Hamsters, as everyone knows, are cute, cuddly, furry little creatures that make ideal pets for children. They take up very little space and are ~~very quiet.~~ ~~totally~~

What a delight they are to watch as they scamper round and round in their little wire wheels exercising their little muscles –

– building them in to massive sprung-steel pile-drivers that will one day be wielded against their hapless owners who have lavished them with munchy bits of nice green lettuce –

– and oh, so crunchy chunks of garden-fresh carrots.

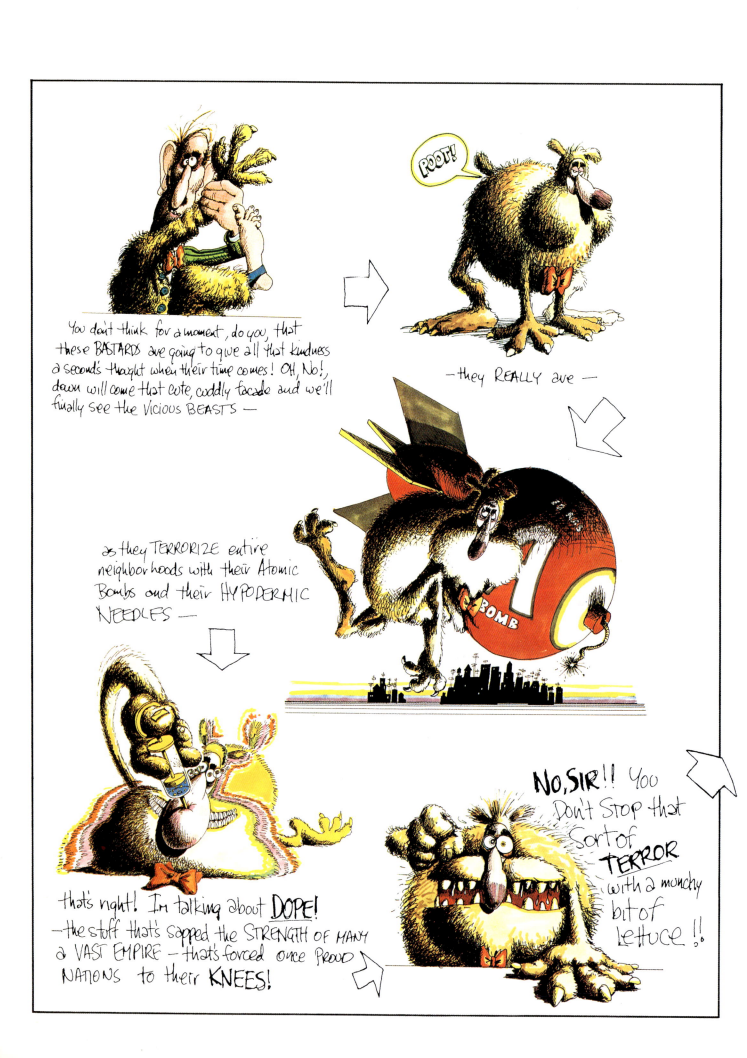

POOT!

You don't think for a moment, do you, that these BASTARDS are going to give all that kindness a second's thought when their time comes! OH, No!, down will come that cute, cuddly facade and we'll finally see the vicious BEASTS —

— they REALLY are —

as they TERRORIZE entire neighborhoods with their Atomic Bombs and their HYPODERMIC NEEDLES —

BOMB

that's right! I'm talking about DOPE! — the stuff that's sapped the STRENGTH OF MANY a VAST EMPIRE — that's forced once PROUD NATIONS to their KNEES!

NO, SIR!! You Don't Stop that Sort of TERROR with a munchy bit of Lettuce !!

Teach Yourself Surgery

Introduced by A Famous Surgeon

I am a famous surgeon. I am more famous than the night-nurse, and much more famous than the silly old anaesthetist, and I am far, far more famous than any hospital orderly or even a ward sister. I am more famous than most junior house doctors, and what's more, more famous than Matron or the Registrar, in his silly little office. In hospital terms I am, thus, very famous indeed. When compared to Stan the Batt I am also famous, and I am also famouser than R. Wilkes. I am probably now more famous than Lita Roza ever was, and, in terms of fame, I probably have the edge on Connie Francis as well. The Lesley Gore revival a year ago made her momentarily more famous than me, but now I am on an equal terms of fame with her and Eve Boswell—and who's ever heard of Annette Funicello since 'Tall Paul'? In fame terms, compared to me, Annette Funicello rates about as high as a small hedge to a big tree. I doubt, myself, whether Annette Funicello would be famous as our anaesthetist, but this is only my own personal view.

Now take Brenda Lee . . .

Another famous surgeon carries on.

I'm sorry about my colleague's endless preoccupation with female vocalists of the late fifties and sixties both here in Britain and in the United States. I prefer Country Music myself, but of all I enjoy being a famous surgeon, and I am very pleased to have been asked to introduce this invaluable article on 'Teaching Yourself Surgery.' For of all, there are some basic Do's and Don'ts which the home surgeon must remember:

Do's

1) Do remember to tie off the ascending aorta well above the left ventricle when removing the heart.
2) Do remember to expose the peri-orbital fascia using a perforator and then a burr to make the opening through the orbitas and splendid plates of the zygomatic bone.
3) Do not use the bread knife

Don'ts

1) Remember to wear a hankie over your face (this should have been in the DO'S).
2) Don't try heart-lung transplants if you're going out in the evening.
3) Don't treat me like a fool.
4) Don't attempt circumcisions after you've had a few.

What you will need for home surgery

Table, two chairs, glass of beer, 100W bulb, cotton-wool, forceps, swabs, waste paper basket, ashtray, sutures, long white coat (cricket flannels will do), breathing apparatus, sponge, blotting paper, absorbent lint, towel, old news-papers, greaseproof paper, a sharp knife, flour, 3 lb potatoes and a record player that takes 78s.

Instructions

V.B. It is very, very important that you follow these instructions. It may be your own kitchen table and your own grapefruit knife, but you are still dealing with Human Life.

1) Clear away the tea things.
2) Make absolutely certain (from the 'Parts Of The Body' Chart) that you know which bit you're going to work on.
3) Undress the patient. (There's nothing rude or dirty about this – surgeons do it all the time.)
4) Put the cat out.
5) Make the incision.
6) Oh, anaesthetise the patient . . . sorry.
7) Do the surgery.
8) If the cat's come in again – THROW IT OUT!
9) Stitch the patient up – often Granny or an aunt can be doing this while you're off having a drink.
10) Clear the table and lay the break-fast.

The Home Surgeon's Parts of the body guide

head
arms
bum
legs
costodiaphragmetre line of reflection of the dura
bronchus principalis
vena cava superior
ventriculus dexter
ventriculus sinister
arteria pulmonalis
right atrioventricula orifice